FROM
COPYING
TO
CREATING

DO NOT WRITE IN THIS BOOK

FROM COPYING TO CREATING

Controlled Compositions and Other Basic Writing Exercises

HELEN HEIGHTSMAN GORDON
Bakersfield College

HOLT, RINEHART AND WINSTON

New York   Chicago   San Francisco   Dallas
Montreal   Toronto   London   Sydney

To my father and mother,
my first and best teachers

Copyright © 1981 by Holt, Rinehart and Winston
All rights reserved
Printed in the United States of America
Published simultaneously in Canada
ISBN: 0-03-053551-4
2 3 4   039   9 8 7 6 5 4 3

Introduction to the Instructor

This textbook combines some new and some traditional approaches to the teaching of basic writing for adults. It uses controlled compositions to give students a maximum amount of actual writing practice while requiring a minimum of grading time by the instructor. It makes limited use of sentence combining for helping students understand such structural matters as compounding and subordinating. At the same time, it retains the quick-reference advantages of a more traditional brief "handbook," to which the instructor can send the student who has serious problems with recurrent common errors. The lessons and handbook are frequently cross-referenced. Also included are numerous suggestions for topics for original compositions.

Controlled compositions are basically imitative writing. Very little grammatical analysis is required, and explanations are worded in the simplest possible terms. The student copies well-written prose passages, changing them in some meaningful way, such as from present to past, singular to plural, and so on. Or he or she combines selected sentences in a passage to form compound sentences, subordinate clauses, and so on. Then the student can apply these skills in his or her own creations, using suggested topics included with each lesson.

This book offers the following advantages for instructors and students:

1. *Flexibility.* The lessons are suitable either for a classroom or a self-paced program, and the methods are effective for students with widely varying abilities.

2. *Relevant and readable content.* Topics appeal to the interests of young adults and college students without alienating the older student. Some examples of topics are nutrition, understanding oneself and others, attitudes needed for success, healthy personality, marriage enhancement, getting and keeping a job, and so on. The reading levels are as simple as the topics will permit.

3. *Confidence-building sequence.* The assignments begin with simple skills like proofreading and become progressively more difficult. Later assignments build upon earlier ones for a reinforcing effect. Because the student concentrates on one skill at a time, chances of error are greatly reduced. The remedial student can have the experience of writing many perfect papers; he or she may rewrite a paper to perfect it or try the same skill on a second controlled composition in the same lesson. Because the student does not have to think of a topic, the writing tasks are nonthreatening. Proofreading is stressed in all lessons to encourage a confident independence and self-mastery.

4. *Sound learning theory.* The principles of immediate feedback and reinforcement apply to controlled compositions because most assignments can be completed and graded in a class hour. Recent theories on brain hemisphericity have also contributed to the methodology. The exercises teach to both halves of the brain by using imitation and manipulation of holistic patterns, and by teaching punctuation in a holistic context (for example, punctuation needed to write dialogue). The learning principle of repetition is also utilized. When necessary, drills to remedy individual problems can be prescribed from the handbook.

If aides, tutors, or readers are available, they can easily check controlled compositions with the aid of the key in the *Instructor's Manual.* For checking the simpler lessons, students may exchange papers. Other suggestions for easing the burdens of grading are offered in the *Instructor's Manual.*

The *Instructor's Manual* may be obtained through a local Holt representative or by writing to the English Editor, College Department, Holt, Rinehart and Winston, 383 Madison Avenue, New York, N.Y. 10017.

The author wishes to thank the following reviewers: Paul G. Bator, Wayne State University; James S. Hill, Oklahoma State University; Myra J. Linden, Joliet Junior College; Phyllis Mehranian, Los Angeles City College; Audrey Roth, Miami-Dade Community College; Bonnie K. Stevens, The College of Wooster.

The author acknowledges with much appreciation the help of many colleagues in developing this textbook, chiefly Dorothy Bray, Nancy McGrath, Lowell Dabbs, and Joyce Lockford. Valuable editorial comment was provided by Richard S. Beal and by the staff of Holt, Rinehart and Winston, particularly Kenney Withers, Lester A. Sheinis, and Maribeth Anderson Payne.

H.H.G.

Contents

DO NOT WRITE IN THIS BOOK

A Brief Handbook for Correcting Errors

FROM
COPYING
TO
CREATING

Introduction to the Student: How to Use This Book

Can you learn to write well without learning a lot of grammar? Yes, if you can read good writing and imitate it. All good writers improve their own writing by seeing how others use the written language, which is similar to spoken language in some ways and different in others. Then, when they want to express their own thoughts in writing, they imitate some of the sentence and paragraph patterns they have observed.

Controlled compositions are a tool for learning to imitate standard written English—that is, the kind that most educated native speakers and writers use. All you do is copy a well-written passage, changing it in some meaningful way such as from present to past, plural to singular, slang to standard English, and so on. The directions will be different for each lesson.

There are various ways in which you and your teacher may use this book. At first, however, you should follow the steps below because they have worked well for others.

1. Read the lesson. Don't skip it, because it tells you what you need to know before doing the exercises.
2. If a sentence-practice exercise comes before the controlled composition, do it first and have your teacher check it. It will help you get ready for the harder assignments following.
3. Do one of the two controlled compositions, either the first one or the one that interests you more. (The second one is sometimes a little harder.) If

you own your book, you may want to mark the places you need to change before writing out the whole passage. But that step isn't really writing, and you learn more by writing the whole thing out. As you write, notice the way punctuation is used and the way good sentences are formed. Later those things you have learned will become automatic in your own writing.

4. Turn in your controlled composition to be checked against the answer key. The boxes you have put around your changes will make it easier to check.

5. If you make more than three errors on the controlled composition, either do it again perfectly or try the other one in the same lesson. Don't do any lesson more than twice, however. Move on.

6. As often as you and your teacher wish, choose one of the suggested topics from the "creating" section in each lesson, and write an original paper. Try to use the skills you have learned from earlier lessons as well.

7. If certain kinds of errors get marked again and again by your teachers, look up the problems in the handbook section at the back of the book. This handbook gives you advice on how to find and correct your own errors. It also contains an exercise for each of the writing problems it covers.

Learning to create with words takes practice, just as any other skill does. But the more you practice, if you are imitating good writing, the more you can enjoy what you create.

LESSON
1

Proofreading and Copying Exactly

Most people can cut their writing errors in half or eliminate them completely by careful proofreading. Proofreading is looking over what you have written, seeing exactly what you have down on paper, and making any changes necessary to make the writing clear to your readers. Because your mind moves faster than your hand, you may have left out some words or letters in your first draft that you can easily spot upon rereading. Or you may think of a better word to use in a particular place. Or you may see a subject and verb that do not agree or punctuation that needs correcting. You may already know how to correct these mistakes if you have been speaking and writing English for a long time.

You may have noticed that it's easier to spot mistakes in someone else's writing than to see them in your own. That's because you still have in your head what you wanted to say, and you may be listening to the words in your head instead of seeing what you put on paper. For that reason, it's best to let some time go by between writing and proofreading—an hour or a day or several days—so the ideas will seem fresh to you. If you can't do that, however, pretend you are the reader instead of the writer. Would everything be clear to you if you had never seen this paper before?

It's also a good idea to read aloud as you proofread. Then you get help from your ears as well as your eyes. If something sounds "funny," double-check it. Listen for the rhythm of the sentences the way you listen to a song. You'll like your writing best when it sounds most pleasing to the ear.

The trick is to see exactly what you are doing. That's important in any kind of learning. In Assignment 1.1, you'll see how a tennis player improved his backhand by first seeing exactly what he was doing.

Controlled Composition 1.1
Copying Exactly and Proofreading

On a separate piece of paper or in your writing notebook, copy the following passage exactly as it appears. Then proofread it to make sure what you wrote is exactly the same, including capitals and punctuation.

Seeing Exactly What Is There
(Adapted from *The Inner Game of Tennis*, by Timothy Gallwey)

Timothy Gallwey, a tennis coach, tells a story about a businessman who came to him for help with his backhand stroke. "I take my racket too high on my backswing," the businessman explained. "Five different tennis pros have told me so, but I haven't been able to correct it."

Gallwey asked the businessman to take a few swings on the patio. His backswing started very low, but then, sure enough, just before swinging forward it lifted to the level of his shoulder and swung down into the imaginary ball. The five pros were right. That stroke would have put a spin on the ball and caused it to sail out of the court. But just telling him that wouldn't help. He had to see it for himself.

Gallwey said, "Why don't you take a closer look at it?" They walked over to a windowpane where the businessman could see his reflection. He swung again, then said in amazement, "Hey, I really do take my racket too high! It goes back up above my shoulder!" He tried again, watching his reflection and feeling the difference in his arm when he kept his racket low. Then Gallwey took him to the court, threw him a few balls, and asked him to remember the feel of that stroke. In ten minutes he was controlling the ball beautifully. He had been worrying so much about what he should do that he hadn't been able to see what he was actually doing. He could change his stroke, but first he had to see it as it was.

Reprinted by permission of the publisher, Random House, Inc.

Controlled Composition 1.2

On a separate piece of paper or in your writing notebook, copy the following passage exactly as it appears. Then proofread it to make sure what you wrote is exactly the same, including capitals and punctuation.

Mistakes and Learning

(Adapted from *The Inner Game of Tennis,* by Timothy Gallwey)

Timothy Gallwey, a tennis coach, teaches his students to accept their mistakes as a necessary part of learning. Once we see our tennis strokes or our written sentences exactly as they are, we can change them. But if we judge them as "bad," we are setting up fears that can keep us from learning more and block us from seeing our work clearly.

Gallwey compares the beginning learner to a plant. When we plant a rose seed in the earth, we notice that it is small, but we do not criticize it as "rootless and stemless." We treat it as a seed, giving it the water and nourishment required of a seed. When it first shoots up out of the earth, we don't say, "Look how immature it is. The buds aren't even open!" We stand in wonder at the process taking place and give the plant the care it needs at each stage of development.

Similarly, beginning tennis players and writers can learn a lot from errors. Errors are not *bad* events, only stages in learning. The first step in getting to the next stage is to see our tennis strokes just as they are, or to see exactly what we have put down on paper.

Reprinted by permission of the publisher, Random House, Inc.

Creating

DO NOT WRITE IN THIS BOOK

1.3   Choose two somewhat similar pictures from a magazine, such as two country scenes or two pictures showing people doing something together. Look closely at the details in one picture, and write a paragraph describing it. Then see if a classmate can pick the right picture after reading your description of it.

1.4   Choose a picture from a magazine or book. Look at the details and write a paragraph describing the picture. Then ask a classmate to draw a picture from your description. How close does he or she come to the original picture? Did you give enough details to help your classmate get a picture in his or her mind?

LESSON
2

Using a and an Correctly

The two words *a* and *an* come before a name of a person or thing to show there is one rather than many (as in "I saw *a man* eating *an apple*."). The words *a* and *an* can also show that the statement applies to anyone or anything (as in the sentence "*A person* should have *an adequate supply* of Vitamin C to treat *a cold*").

We use the word *an* when the following word begins with a vowel letter (the vowels are *a, e, i, o,* and *u*). Examples are *an apple, an efficient worker, an idea, an orange,* or *an uncle.* We use the word *a* before the vowel *u* when it is pronounced as "u," however, as in *a uniform, a useful tool.* We also use the word *an* before words that begin with silent *h* (for example, *an honest man* or *an honor*) but not when the *h* is pronounced, as in *a human being* or *a hard job.*

We use the word *a* before words that begin with consonant sounds (that is, all sounds that are not vowels), as in *a banana* or *a fried egg.*

Controlled Composition 2.1
Practice with *a* and *an*

Copy all of the following passage in your notebook, making the changes listed below. Put a box around each of your changes, proofread the whole paper to make sure it sounds right to you, and then see your instructor to compare your paper to the answer key. To help you find the places that need changing, they are underlined in the passage. Use *a* or *an* as needed along with these changes:

In sentence 1, change <u>teacher</u> to <u>instructor</u>.
In sentence 2, change <u>teacher</u> to <u>instructor</u> and <u>adventurer</u> to <u>seeker</u>.
In sentence 3, change <u>honest teacher</u> to <u>curious teacher</u>.
In sentence 6, change <u>task</u> to <u>assignment</u>.
In sentence 12, change <u>learner</u> to <u>eager learner</u>.
In sentence 13, change <u>new light</u> to <u>different way</u>.

Your first sentence, when changed, will look like this:

| An instructor | is a student's partner in learning.

What Is a Teacher?

(1) A <u>teacher</u> is a student's partner in learning. (2) A <u>teacher</u> is an <u>adventurer</u>—skilled in the learning arts, comfortable about the discomfort of changes, challenged by the unknown. (3) An <u>honest teacher</u> says, "I don't know; let's find out." (4) An effective teacher shares. (5) A caring teacher listens. (6) If you don't know how to do a <u>task</u>, a teacher shows you how. (7) If you think you don't care, a teacher cares enough for both of you.

(8) Mothers and fathers are teachers. (9) Friends are teachers. (10) A teacher can be anybody who cares or listens or shows you how or tells you something new. (11) A student can be a teacher, too; friends and teachers learn by watching the student learn.

(12) A teacher is always a <u>learner</u>. (13) A teacher identifies with the searching minds of students, and through their eyes the teacher often sees the world in a <u>new light</u>. (14) When they succeed, the teacher succeeds, too. (15) That's why a student is a teacher's partner in learning.

Controlled Composition 2.2

Copy all of the following passages in your notebook, making the changes listed below. Use *a* or *an* as needed along with the changes. Put a box around each of your changes, proofread the whole paper, and then have your instructor compare your paper to the answer key. To help you find the places that need changing, they are underlined in the passage.

In sentence 1, change applicant to person, background to history, unwillingness to reluctance, and high to unrealistic.

In sentence 2, change management-level to executive; change survey to report.

In sentence 3, change lack of experience to inadequate background.

In sentence 4, change advantage to special advantage; change position to job.

In sentence 5, change poor to bad.

In sentence 6, change bad to unfavorable.

In sentence 7, change interest to keen interest; change willingness to eagerness.

Your first sentence, when changed, will look like this:

If   a person   doesn't get a job he or she is well qualified for, the reason is probably one of these four: (and so on)

Nine Reasons for Not Getting Hired

(1) If an applicant doesn't get a job he or she is well qualified for, the reason is probably one of these four: a background of job-hopping, an unwillingness to move to a new city, a personality that clashes with the potential employer's personality, or a high salary demand. (2) Those are the four main reasons for turning down an applicant for a management-level job, according to a survey by National Personnel Network. (3) The fifth reason is a lack of experience for that type of work. (4) The applicant may need to prove that the experience he or she does have provides an advantage over the usual type of training for such a position. (5) The sixth reason is a poor employment record. (6) The applicant may need to explain a bad reference from a former employer. (7) A person may also be turned down if he or she doesn't show an interest in the work, a willingness to take responsibility, and a proven ability to get along well with others.

Creating

2.3 Write a paragraph about a day's meals with these items on the menu, using *a* and *an* correctly before them. Breakfast: egg, slice of bacon, piece of toast, glass of milk, orange. Lunch: avocado and tomato salad, bowl of vegetable soup, cup of tea. Dinner: small shrimp cocktail, enormous steak, eggplant side dish, apple cobbler, cup of coffee.

2.4 Write a paragraph about the requirements for success in these careers, using *a* and *an* correctly: engineer, businessman (or businesswoman), educator, artist, doctor, electrician, welder, carpenter.

2.5 Think about the following quotation: "The difference between an amateur and a professional photographer is that the professional has a fuller wastebasket." Then write a paragraph comparing an amateur and a professional in some kind of work, activity, or sport that you know a lot about. Use *a* and *an* correctly.

LESSON
3

Writing About Men and Women

We use the pronouns *he, him, his,* and *himself* to refer to a man. (There is no such word as *hisself.*) We use *she, her, hers,* and *herself* to refer to a woman.

Controlled Composition 3.1
Practice Writing About Men and Women

Rewrite this passage in your own notebook, changing it so that it describes a woman instead of a man. Put a box around each of your changes, proofread the whole paper to be sure it makes sense, and then see your instructor to compare your paper to the answer key. Pronouns you will need to change are underlined. Your first sentence, when changed, will look like this:

The healthy personality is a person who likes | herself. |

The Healthy Personality

   The healthy personality is a person who likes himself. He likes other people and accepts their faults as well as his own. He acts naturally, without pretending to be anything he is not. He prefers to face an unpleasant reality rather than retreat to a pleasant fantasy. Usually his behavior is like that of his friends, but he can be different if necessary. His moral values are the highest; he wants justice and fairness for all people. Being alone is no problem for him, and he stays true to his beliefs even when all others seem to be against him.

He feels a sense of belonging to mankind as a whole, so he does not discriminate against people because of race, social class, or religion. When he sees an injustice, he is likely to speak out against it. Although he enjoys the company of others, he is not dependent on them. Close friends of his make up a comparatively small group, but their relationship to him is deep, meaningful, and lasting. He has a tender love for children. And like a child, he sees the world freshly; he can appreciate again and again the beauty in ordinary things—a sunset, a flower, a baby, a person.

Controlled Composition 3.2

Rewrite this whole passage in your notebook, but change it so that it describes a woman instead of a man. Put a box around each of your changes, proofread the whole paper to be sure it makes sense, and then have your instructor compare your paper to the answer key. The pronouns you will need to change are underlined. Your first sentence, when changed, will look like this:

It's easy to understand why | **a woman** | would fear failure.

Fear of Success

It's easy to understand why a man would fear failure. It's harder to understand why a man would fear success. But many men do. If his friends are better than he is at throwing frisbees or getting dates, a man may decide at a young age that fate intends him to be at the bottom of the pile in everything. And how can he fight such a big thing as fate? On the other hand, if his friends are not as good as he is, he may feel guilty about passing them up. Does he really deserve an *A* in biology, when they get only *C*'s; or a job at $5.00 an hour when they earn only $3.00? Surely, he tells himself, no one will love him if he gets too far ahead of the crowd.

He looks around <u>him</u>. Would it be right for <u>him</u> to be better educated than his parents or his spouse? Education will change <u>him</u>, and they might not like hearing <u>him</u> speak differently or think differently. So <u>he</u> holds <u>himself</u> back, afraid <u>he</u> might rock the boat. He settles into a comfortable rut, but <u>he</u> often wonders whether <u>he</u> is getting all <u>he</u> should out of life.

Creating

3.3   Write a paragraph about a man or a woman you don't like, telling enough about what he or she has done so that the reader can see why you don't like him or her. Use the proper pronouns throughout your paper—*he, him, himself, his,* or *she, her, herself, hers.*

3.4   Write a paragraph about a man or a woman you want to be like, giving enough reasons so the reader can see why you admire him or her. Use the proper pronouns thoughout your paper.

LESSON
4

*Writing About More
Than One Person*

Notice the differences in these two sentences:

1. A valued customer pays his bills promptly.
2. Valued customers pay their bills promptly.

In the second sentence, the word *a* was dropped and three words changed (from *customer/pays/his* to *customers/pay/their*). All these changes may be necessary when we write about more than one person. This is called making the sentence plural.

The name of a person, place, or thing is called a noun, and we make most nouns plural by adding *s* or *-es*. Examples: *one peach/two peaches*, and *one car/two cars*. A few common words have special kinds of endings to make them plural. Examples: *one child/two children; one man/two men; one alumnus/ two alumni*. Other examples may be found in the handbook section on nouns and noun plurals.

Plural subjects (always nouns) require plural verbs, which usually do *NOT* end in *s*. Examples: *One car runs; two cars run. One woman thinks; two women think*. Some common verbs also have special forms to make them plural. Examples: one baby *does* cry; all babies *do* cry. One lady *is* nice; two ladies *are* nice. One man *wasn't* to blame; two men *weren't* to blame.

Pronouns also change to refer to more than one person or thing. Examples: *He* paints *his* house by *himself*. *She* paints *her* house by *herself*. But to write about both of them we would say *They* paint *their* house by *themselves*. (NOTE: the words *theirselves* and *hisself* are not considered standard English and should not be used in writing.)

When something belongs to more than one person, we say it is *theirs* or it belongs to *them*.

We say that the subject and verb are in *agreement* when both are singular or both are plural. Pronouns must also *agree* with the nouns they refer to (for example, customers would be referred to as *they*).

Controlled Composition 4.1
Practice Writing About One Person

Copy the following passage in your own notebook, changing it so it describes more than one person. Remember that several people can have one need. Put a box around each of your changes, proofread the whole paper to be sure it is consistently plural, and then have your instructor compare your paper to the answer key. Your first sentence, when changed, will look like this:

Competitors see so much competition in American society that they think it is a law of nature.

The Competitor
(Adapted from *Why Am I Afraid to Tell You Who I Am?* by John Powell)

The competitor sees so much competition in American society that he thinks it is a law of nature. He thinks nothing is more important than winning. He turns everything into a "win or lose" situation. In conversation, he doesn't discuss; he debates and argues. The victories that he seeks, so often at the expense of hurting others, may be intended to make up for a lack of approval in his childhood. His early doubts have left him thinking that he isn't worth much. So he tries to prove his importance by putting others down. His need to be noticed intensifies his drive to get ahead. He becomes angry with anyone who achieves more than he does. Sooner or later, he will be overcome by a sense of failure, since his appetite for victory becomes harder and harder to satisfy. What he needs to learn is that his own worth is separate from the worth of his achievements. There is room for all kinds of excellence in the world, and other people's achievements take nothing away from his. When he realizes that, he can be pleased with the successes of others, and others will return the respect he gives to them.

Reprinted from *Why Am I Afraid to Tell You Who I Am?* by John S. Powell, © 1969 Argus Communications. Used with permission from Argus Communications, Niles, Illinois.

Controlled Composition 4.2

Rewrite the following passage in your notebook, changing the person described to two people. That is, change "my dad" (singular) to "my parents" (plural), and make any other changes necessary to describe both parents as punsters (jokers). However, don't make the other persons plural (their child or the friend), and don't change the wording of the jokes in quotation marks. Be especially careful in the fifth sentence with the words *they're* (they are) and *their* (belonging to them). Other pronouns you will need are *they, we, them, themselves,* and *theirs*.

Put a box around each of your changes, proofread the whole paper to be sure it makes sense, and have your instructor compare your paper to the answer key. Sentence 1, when changed, will look like this:

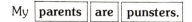

My parents are punsters.

My Dad the Joker

My dad is a punster. He amuses himself with corny puns like this one: "Have you heard that the students are revolting? Some of them are more revolting than others." This old favorite of his might pop up at any mealtime: "Do you carrot all for me? My heart beets for you. If we cantaloupe, lettuce marry anyhow." He asks his friends questions like this one: "How's your broom-mate—the one you're sweeping with?" He thinks he's clever when he makes up his own puns like this one: "How can you fluff up a down pillow? Why, it's eiderdown. It fluffs eider down or up." When my little sister was born on Halloween, he said, "That's just what we wanted—a little ghoul for Halloween." I groan a lot when my dad makes jokes like that. But once a friend of mine said, "I'm glad my parents don't have a sense of humor." He meant, of course, that he envied me. I still groan so my dad knows I heard his corny jokes, but secretly I'm glad I have him for a parent.

Creating

4.3 Write a paragraph on the topic "Cats (or Dogs) Are Like People," using plural subjects and plural verbs throughout the paper.

4.4 Write on the topic "People Are Like Sheep," using plural subjects and verbs throughout, giving examples of people behaving like sheep.

4.5   Think about this quotation: "Good parents are like turtles—hard on the outside and soft on the inside." Then write about your own parents (or your own experiences, if you are a parent), using plural subjects, verbs, and pronouns wherever possible.

4.6   Complete this statement with a word or phrase: "The members of my family are _____." (For example, *generous, loving, loyal, selfish, quarrelsome, weird, funny.*) Then write a paragraph explaining why you think that word or phrase describes them. Use plural subjects, verbs, and pronouns in order to write about them as a group.

LESSON
5

Writing About One Person

The assignments in Lesson 5 are the reverse, or opposite, of the assignments in Lesson 4. You are to change a passage from plural to singular (that is, writing about a single person or thing). We use the words *one, he, his, him,* and *himself* to write about one person if the person is male or if the person could be of either sex.

Some writers are not comfortable using *he* and *his* for a person of either sex. They prefer to use *he or she, him or her, he/she,* and *him/her.* Other writers feel that such combinations are awkward. A few writers are even using *she, her, hers,* and *herself* when writing about a person of either sex. They are trying to change a part of the language that they feel has been unfair. But changing the habits of language takes a long time, so most writers still use *he* to mean a person of either sex.

Because they are not comfortable with using *he* for either sex, more and more people are using expressions like these:

Someone left *their* pen.
Does *anyone* want *their* coffee cup refilled?
Everyone took *their* places.

In the past, we have always considered words ending in *one* to be singular, and we would use *his* instead of *their.* Spoken language changes faster than written language, so although you will hear such expressions quite often, you might be safer to use *his or her* in such sentences when you write.

Remember that singular subjects need singular verbs, so you will be changing verbs to singular form whenever you change subjects to singular form. For example, people *make* mistakes; a person *makes* mistakes. Never change forms like *to do* or *to be afraid;* these are not verbs, but nouns or modifiers that look like verbs. The best test of a verb is whether it can be put into the past tense. You will learn more about this in Lesson 8. Meanwhile, don't change anything with *to* in front of it.

Controlled Composition 5.1
Practice Writing About One Person

Rewrite this passage in your own notebook. Change it so that it describes one person. Remember that one person can make several mistakes. Put a box around each of your changes, proofread to make sure the whole paper makes sense, and then have your instructor check your paper against the answer key. Your first sentence, when changed, will look like this:

An indecisive person   is   one who cannot make decisions for fear of making mistakes. The greatest mistake   he   can make . . .

Indecisive People
(Adapted from *Why Am I Afraid to Tell You Who I Am?* by John Powell)

Indecisive people are those who cannot make decisions for fear of making mistakes. The greatest mistake they can make is to be afraid of making mistakes. Their uncertainty keeps them from taking responsibilities; they think if no decision is made nothing can go wrong. Sometimes they drag out making necessary decisions as long as possible, which can be annoying to their families or people they work with.

Their basic problem is self-esteem. They fear they might lose respect if their decisions turn out to be wrong. But all of us are wrong sometimes. Only little men, someone has said, are never wrong. Bigger men take more chances and make more mistakes, but they learn from those mistakes and so they have more successes, too.

Very often, indecisive people are trying to think of too many things at once. In that case, they may find it helpful to make a list of things to do, take the most important tasks first, and cross them off one by one as they get them done.

Reprinted from *Why Am I Afraid to Tell You Who I Am?* by John S. Powell, © 1969 Argus Communications. Used with permission from Argus Communications, Niles, Illinois.

Controlled Composition 5.2

Rewrite this passage in your own notebook, but change it so that it describes one person. Put a box around each of your changes, proofread, and then have your instructor check your paper against the answer key. Your first sentence, when changed, will look like this:

The system-beater is a person who uses up a lot of time and energy trying to beat the system.

The System-Beaters

The system-beaters are persons who use up a lot of time and energy trying to beat the system. They try to use phony money in vending machines, even when they have the real money to buy what they need. On the job, they ask other workers to punch their time cards when they are not there. In school, they cut classes and then lie about why they were absent. They turn in the work of others and say it is theirs. They think they are very clever about getting out of work.

But eventually the system-beaters pay a great price for their cleverness. Their fellow workers and employers do not trust them because, if they cheat on their time cards, they are likely to cheat in other ways. Without trust and respect, they are not likely to get promoted to a better job.

In school, they waste time that they could spend learning, and then they have to work even harder to try to cover up what they do not know. If they later try to go to college, they may have to spend a year or more of extra time to learn what they should have learned many years before. In the long run, they have not saved any time or energy. They have only hurt themselves.

Creating

5.3 Write a paragraph about one person you know who made a mistake, telling whether he or she handled it well or badly. Use singular subjects, verbs, and pronouns to write about this one person. If the person is female, use *she, her, hers,* and *herself.*

5.4 You are also writing about one person when you write about yourself. Write on the topic "A Mistake I Learned Something From," using *I, me, myself,* and *mine* for pronouns. Use singular verbs to go with them.

LESSON
6

Using You Consistently

Informal language is the kind we use in everyday conversation. Formal language is the kind we use in speeches, at funerals, in college term papers, and on dignified occasions. Compare the following two sentences that say the same thing, but in different words:

1. Mother says it is quite expensive to buy children's clothing.
2. Mom says it's very expensive to buy clothes for the kids.

Both sentences are good English, but the first is more formal, and the second is more informal. Contractions like *it's* (for *it is*) and *won't* (for *will not*) are usually informal.

When we want a message to sound personal and informal, we can address our reader directly as "you." When we do, we should use the words *you, your, yourself,* and *yours* consistently all through the paper. The words *you are* can be written as *you're* in informal writing. Here is an example of using *you* forms consistently:

You should turn your papers in to *your* teachers on time so *you* don't lose points for being late.

Below is an example of inconsistent use of pronouns. The writer wanders back and forth between using *I* forms and *you* forms, even though not discussing two different people:

Inconsistent: *I* turn *my* papers in to *my* teacher on time because *you* lose points if *you* turn *your* paper in late.

Improved: *I* turn *my* papers in to *my* teacher on time because *I* lose points if *I* turn *my* paper in late.

Notice how verbs are used with *you:*

he is	you are	he doesn't	you don't
he was	you were	he can go	you can go
he thinks	you think	he will come	you will come

Controlled Composition 6.1
Practice in Using *You* Consistently

DO NOT WRITE IN THIS BOOK

Rewrite this passage in your own notebook. Change it from a formal passage using *one* and *he* to an informal passage using *you*. Be consistent all through the paper (that is, don't use both *you* and *he* to mean the same person). Put a box around each change you make, proofread to make sure you have been consistent, and have your instructor compare your paper to the answer key. Your first sentence, when changed, will look like this:

If ⬚you⬚ ⬚are⬚ hypnotized and told that ⬚you⬚ ⬚are⬚ at the North Pole, ⬚you⬚ will not only shiver and appear cold, but also develop goose bumps.

The Secret of Hypnotic Power
(Adapted from *Psycho-Cybernetics,* by Maxwell Maltz)

If one is hypnotized and told that he is at the North Pole, he will not only shiver and appear cold, but also develop goose bumps. The same amazing thing happens if he is told to imagine that one hand is being held under ice water; his temperature will drop in that hand. When he is convinced that the hypnotist's statements are true, he behaves differently because he thinks and believes differently. When he is convinced that he cannot feel pain, he can even have surgery without an anesthetic.

He acts and feels, not according to what things are really like, but according to the image his mind holds of what they are like. He has certain mental images of himself, his world, and the people around him, and he behaves as if these images were true. If one sees himself as clumsy, he will behave in clumsy ways. If he sees himself as a poor speller, his spelling will surely be poor. On the other hand, if he believes he can learn, he will work at learning and succeed at it. In short, whether he thinks he can or cannot do something, he is right.

From the book *Psycho-Cybernetics* by Maxwell Maltz, M.D. © 1960 by Prentice-Hall, Inc. Published by Prentice-Hall, Inc., Englewood Cliffs, New Jersey 07632.

Controlled Composition 6.2

The passage below would be better if it spoke to the reader as "you," directly and personally. Change it from a formal passage using *one* and *he* to an informal passage using *you*. Be consistent all through the paper. Put a box around each of your changes, proofread for consistency, and then have your instructor compare your answer to the answer key. Your first sentence, when changed, will look like this:

As a college student, | you | should read books at about 400 or 500 words per minute.

Speeding Up Reading

As a college student, one should read books at about 400 or 500 words per minute. One can easily increase his reading speed by following a few simple rules. First, he should build his vocabulary by looking up any new words he finds in all the reading he does. The more words he knows, the faster he can read. Next, he should read for ideas, not word by word. He should group words into phrases, according to their meaning. His eyes can easily take in three or four words at one glance. He can also increase the speed of his eye fixations (or stops). If he moves fast enough, he won't be able to say words aloud. Speed also makes it easier for him to relate the ideas in one paragraph to the ideas in the next one. So the faster he goes, the better he will understand what he reads. With practice, he will soon develop a smooth, fast rhythm across the lines and down the page. Using his hand as a pacer may help. He can skim up to 1,000 words a minute by reading only the first and last sentences of each paragraph. But skimming should not be used for studying, only for a quick survey, a general impression, or a review.

Creating

6.3   Using the *you* forms to address your reader, give directions for building, making, or cooking something. Be careful not to use *I;* say instead, "*You* do this and then that." Sometimes when *you* is the subject, it can be understood rather than written. For example, you can say, "Do this," meaning "You do this."

6.4   Using the *you* forms consistently throughout your paper, give directions for getting to a certain place in your city or to some other town. Remember not to use *I* in this paper; use *you* as if you were talking directly to your reader.

LESSON
7

Using One/He/ Him/Himself

In formal writing (as in college papers, reports, and most business letters), the words *one, he, him, his,* and *himself* are preferred over the informal *you* forms. (The informal style was explained in Lesson 6.)

Of course, it is right to use *you* and *your* if these words actually mean the reader, as in these examples:

I will call you next week. Will you be at home?
We received your letter. Thank you for your help.

But when we are writing about people in general, formal language would prefer sentence 2 below to sentence 1 below:

1. You have to find out who you really are.
2. One has to find out who he really is.

Using the word *one* too many times can sound stuffy, so we use *one* near the beginning of a passage and refer back to it with *he* or *him*. Better still, we can use a specific noun instead of *one,* as in these examples:

If *a person* is applying for a job, he can rehearse the interview in his mind.
Knowing that he will be out of town, *a voter* can get an absentee ballot and vote ahead of time.
When he has been ill, *a student* should make up the work he missed.

As explained in Lesson 5, some writers wish to stress that *he* means either a man or a woman and will use *he or she* or *him or her* in place of *he* and *him*. Others consider that awkward and feel safer with the traditional *he*. Language is changing now to recognize changing attitudes toward women, so you can expect to see changing uses of pronouns. If you wish, you may use the forms *he or she* and *him or her* in controlled compositions 7.1 and 7.2.

Remember that verbs must agree with their subjects. In changing the subject from *you* to *he* or *she*, you must change the verb, too.

Controlled Composition 7.1
Practice with *One/He/Him/Himself*

Rewrite the passage below in your own notebook, using the formal pronouns *one, he, him* and *himself* in place of the informal pronoun *you.* Remember not to overuse the word *one*; use it only at the beginning of the passage and refer back to it afterwards with *he* or *he or she.* For examples of whole passages written with *one* and *he,* look back to Assignments 6.1 and 6.2.

Put a box around each of your changes, proofread to make sure you have been consistent with your pronouns, and then have your instructor compare your paper to the answer key. Your first sentence, when changed, will look like this:

Realizing that one's actions, feelings, and behavior are the result of **his** own images and beliefs can give one a new tool for gaining skill, growth, and happiness.

Imagine Yourself Successful
(Adapted from *Psycho-Cybernetics,* by Maxwell Maltz)

Realizing that your actions, feelings, and behavior are the result of your own images and beliefs can give you a new tool for gaining skill, growth, and happiness. Mental pictures give you a chance to practice new attitudes. Your nervous system cannot tell the difference between an actual experience and one that is vividly imagined. If you picture yourself doing something in a certain way, it is nearly the same as actually doing it. Mental practice helps to make your performance more perfect.

If you are a salesman, for example, you can picture yourself in a selling situation, think about what you might say, and solve problems ahead of time. Then you will know what to do and say when the real situation comes up. If you are applying for a job, you can rehearse the interview in your mind. Even if none of the questions you have rehearsed come up in the interview, you will feel more confident.

Mental picturing produces amazing results because the human mind is like an automatic machine that steers its way to a target. But first it must have a target to shoot at. When you see a goal clearly in your mind, the "success mechanism" within you takes over and gets you there.

From the book *Psycho-Cybernetics* by Maxwell Maltz, M.D. © 1960 by Prentice-Hall, Inc. Published by Prentice-Hall, Inc., Englewood Cliffs, New Jersey 07632.

Controlled Composition 7.2

Follow the same directions as for Assignment 7.1. Your first sentence, when changed, will look like this:

If one is a creative job seeker, he will not get discouraged by high unemployment rates nor take the first job he can get.

The Creative Job Seeker

If you are a creative job seeker, you will not get discouraged by high unemployment rates nor take the first job you can get. First, you will decide that you are the one in charge of your life—not some mysterious force called the "job market." Second, you decide exactly what you want to do. You make lists of things you enjoy and don t enjoy, skills you have for working with things and with people, and goals you want to reach. You plan for several career options, because opportunities may be quite different in the future.

Third, you decide where you want to work—large city or small town, in an office or out of doors, and so on. You must know yourself—your needs, your feelings, and what kind of environment would make you happiest. Fourth, you really study all the organizations in the area where you want to work. You talk to people to learn what these organizations are like and what they need. Then you are ready for the fifth step—approaching the one person in each organization who has the power to hire you in the job you want and convincing this person you can contribute something to that company. You may not always succeed with Plan A, but your chances are better this way. And you can always switch to Plan B.

Creating

7.3   Think about this quotation: "Every man is the architect of his own fortune." Because an architect designs buildings and because *fortune* can mean any kind of fate (good or bad), the quotation means that *every man makes his own luck*. Based on your knowledge of people, write a paragraph about how a person makes his own luck. Use *one, he, him, his,* and *himself* in your paragraph. Do not use *you.*

7.4   Think about this quotation: "He has only himself to blame." Then write about how a person can make his own problems or prevent himself from getting what he wants most. Use words like *a person, one, he, him, his,* and *himself.* Do not use *you.*

7.5   Write on either of the above topics, but use *one, she, her,* and *herself* instead of *he, him,* and *himself.* Do not use *you.*

LESSON
8

Changing from Present to Past

Notice how these two sentences differ:

1. I practice daily so I can increase my speed.
2. I practiced daily so I could increase my speed.

One of these sentences tells about what happened in the past. To put an event in the past, we change the verb or the verb helpers (helpers are words like *can, will, may, is, have, has*). In fact, the best way of checking to see if a word is a verb is to try putting it in the past. If we can't do that, it isn't a verb.

To put most verbs in the past, we add *-ed* to the end of the word. Examples are *need/needed, look/looked*. But irregular verbs have special forms. Examples are *is/was, are/were, stand/stood, give/gave, sleep/slept*. There are many more, but if you have been speaking English for several years, you probably know them without having to drill on them. You do need to watch for them in proofreading to make sure you are using the right form. For more details and examples of irregular verbs, see the handbook section of this book entitled "Verb Tenses and Forms."

Some verbs look the same in both present and past. Examples are *put* and *read*, though the word *read* in the past is pronounced like "red."

When the verb has helpers, we can often change them into a past form without changing the rest of the words in the complete verb. Examples: I *am* thinking; I *was* thinking. Today nobody *can* go. Yesterday nobody *could* go. We *think* the plan *may* work; we *thought* the plan *might* work.

Words ending in *-ing* are not always part of a verb. When they are, they always have helpers like *am, is,* or *was,* and only the helper is changed into the past. Never change the *-ing* word itself.

Also, when the word *to* is put before a verb, the phrase so formed no longer functions as a verb. Examples are *to read, to look over, to remember.* The *to* turns the former verb into a noun or a modifier, neither of which can be put into the past tense. For example, in the sentence "I like to read," the past tense would be "I *liked* to read." The verb is *like,* and *to read* is a noun, or the name of what is liked.

One sentence in Assignment 8.1 requires special treatment. In the present it reads: "It's *easy* to fool myself into thinking that if I understand what I read, I am sure to remember it." When changed into the past, it should read: "It was easy to fool myself into thinking that if I understood what I was reading, I would be sure to remember it."

Controlled Composition 8.1
Changing from Present to Past

Pretend that you have graduated from school and are writing the passage below to someone who is just beginning. In your notebook, rewrite the whole passage in the past tense. Put a box around each of your changes, proofread to be sure the whole passage is in the past, and have your instructor check your paper against the answer key. Your first sentence, when changed, will look like this:

When I `was` in school, I `needed` to read for information, not for escape nor entertainment.

Reading to Remember

When I am in school, I need to read for information, not for escape nor entertainment. For school and for my job, I need to remember what I read. So I use the method that helps me remember best.

First, I take about one minute to look over the whole chapter or article, glancing at the title, the pictures, and any other headings or words that stand out from the others. This one-minute survey gives me a general idea what is coming—like looking at a road map before I take a trip. Next, I ask myself questions about what I hope to learn. Asking questions is the best way to make sure I am really thinking about the ideas and not just looking at the words. Then I read carefully, looking for the answers to those questions as I read. It's easy to fool myself into thinking that if I understand what I am reading, I am sure to remember it. But that isn't true. To make sure, I close the book after each section and put the ideas into my own words. Last, I scan the whole chapter or article to review it. That pulls all the pieces together into a meaningful whole, making it easier to remember.

Controlled Composition 8.2

Pretend that you have graduated from college and are giving advice to someone just beginning about how you managed your time. In your notebook, rewrite the whole passage in the past tense. Put a box around each of your changes, proofread, and have your instructor check your paper against the answer key.

Here are some irregular verbs you will need to use: *mean /meant, choose / chose, lead /led, write /wrote, have /had, come /came, fall /fell, take /took, make /made, do /did, try /tried, leave /left, keep /kept.* Remember also that, if the verb includes an *-ing* word, you change only the helper verb and not the *-ing* word. Your first sentence, when changed, will look like this:

Because I wanted to do well in school, I managed my time carefully.

How I Manage My Time

Because I want to do well in school, I manage my time carefully. I avoid the extremes of being too busy (overorganized) and too loose (lazy, disorganized). I decide what my long-range goals are; then I choose the activities that best lead to those goals. I write on my calendar those deadlines I have no control over, such as dates when tests come up, papers fall due, or special events take place. I allow whatever time I need to get prepared for those events. For the time I have left over, I list all the things I need to do to reach my goals, such as studying, exercising, improving a skill, and so on. I make a daily list of those things plus necessary routine tasks like car repairs, shopping, and so on. I put an *A, B,* or *C* beside each item and do the *A*'s first, the *B*'s next, and so on. Every day I change the list, adding or taking away items, changing some from *C* to *B,* and so on. When conflicts come up, I balance them by taking turns or giving more time to an item one day and less the next. I leave at least an hour every day for unexpected things, and I keep all plans flexible in case of emergencies.

Creating

8.3   Talk to a person you know over the age of sixty. Find out what he or she remembers about the "good old days." Were they better or worse than modern times? Then write a paragraph about "What the Good Old Days Were Really Like," using the past tense.

8.4   Write in the past tense about a person you knew long ago but will never forget. Explain what makes that person so unusual.

8.5   Write about the proudest moment of your life, using the past tense.

LESSON
9

Changing from Present to Future

Notice how these two sentences differ:

1. He is in law school and his wife works to help him through.
2. He will be in law school and his wife will work to help him through.

The second sentence tells about a future situation. It uses *he will be* in place of *he is* and uses *she will work* in place of *she works*. We can write about the future in two ways, using *will* or *going to*. It is all right to say informally, "I'm going to be graduating in June," but in a letter or college paper we would be more likely to write, "I will be graduating in June."

Words like *not, always, also,* and *surely* can come between *will* and *be,* as in "I *will always be* grateful."

When using *he, she,* or *it,* we must often drop an *s* as we add *will.*

Examples: It *makes* life easy.   It *will make* life easy.
             He *understands*.   He *will understand*.
             She *tries* hard.   She *will try* hard.

Dependent clauses like those underlined in Assignments 9.1 and 9.2 serve as modifiers and are not changed into future form. Only the verbs in the main clause are changed. You will learn more about dependent clauses in Lessons 11 and 12. Meanwhile, do not change the clauses underlined in Assignments 9.1 and 9.2.

Controlled Composition 9.1
Practice Changing from Present to Future

Pretend that you have not yet started college but are making plans for being a good student when you get there. Rewrite the following passage, putting it into the future. Remember that you will *not* make any changes in the clauses that are underlined. Put a box around each of your changes, proofread to be sure the whole paper makes sense, and have your instructor check it against the answer key. Your first sentence, when changed, will look like this:

Succeeding in college   will not be   a matter of luck.

A Success Formula for College

Succeeding in college is not a matter of luck. I follow a fail-proof system. To begin with, I take only the number of units that I can handle in the time I have. I take no more than twelve units with a part-time job, and no more than six units with a full-time job. I go to class every single day unless I am sick. I listen carefully to the instructor and try to follow his instructions exactly. If I do not understand his instructions clearly, I ask him to explain some more.

My class notes include only the most important things that the teacher says. It is impossible to write down every word, and that is not necessary anyway. I make sure, however, to write down what he puts on the board because he must consider that important. I reread my notes as soon as possible to fix the ideas in my memory.

I read my assigned homework before going to class, so I understand in advance what the teacher is talking about. Also, I know ahead of time whether I need to ask the instructor questions about the textbook. Learning the textbook material before class also makes it easier to take notes in class. I never just guess on practice exercises, hoping that, with luck, I will get them right. I really think about them. Then I really learn them and remember them.

Controlled Composition 9.2

Pretend that you have recently learned how to handle depression and are telling a friend how you expect to handle it in the future. Rewrite the following passage, putting it into the future. Remember that you will *not* make any changes in the clauses that are underlined. Put a box around each of your changes, proofread to be sure the whole paper makes sense, and have your instructor check it with the answer key. Your first sentence, when changed, will look like this:

| If I get depressed in the future, | I | will | know how to help myself.

Handling Depression

When I am depressed, I know how to help myself. I accept the fact that some depression is normal. I am not able to control such depressing things as bad weather, hormone changes in my body, or grief over the loss of a loved one. I deal with those kinds of depression by accepting them and telling myself they will pass in time. Reading, movies, and television give me some temporary relief from a dark mood.

But other kinds of depression need a different approach. I check my diet to see if too much sugar or caffeine might be giving me "sugar blues." I also increase my protein foods, whole grain cereals, and fresh fruits. If I feel lonely, I talk to a friend. If I feel rejected, I remind myself that the one who rejects me probably has more problems than I have. For hate causes depression, too, when it turns in upon ourselves.

I try not to keep negative feelings inside me very long because they make me depressed. Talking to trusted friends helps, or seeing a counselor helps. But I do not let depression get me down for long.

Creating

9.3 Reverend Jesse Jackson has inspired many people with the words, "If you can conceive it and believe it, you can achieve it." Write a paragraph about what you want your life to be like ten years from now—what work you will be doing, what people will be important in your life, how you will be spending your leisure time, and so on.

9.4   Martin Luther King, Jr., began a famous speech with the words, "I have a dream." Tell what dreams you have for a better world in the future.

9.5   Pretend you have just received notice that you will inherit a million dollars sometime soon. Write about what you will do in the future when you have a million dollars to spend.

9.6   Write about the home you would like to have someday. Give enough details about it so your reader can picture it in his mind. Use the future tense because you don't have the home yet.

LESSON
10

Combining to Make Compound Sentences

When the ideas in two sentences are related, we can join them together as a compound sentence. See how this is done:

TWO SENTENCES: I know Harry well. I trust him.
COMPOUND SENTENCES:
   I know Harry well, *and* I trust him.
   I know Harry well, *so* I trust him.
   I know Harry well, *but* I don't trust him.
   I do not know Harry very well, *yet* I trust him.
   I do not know Harry very well, *nor* do I trust him.
   Either we trust Harry, *or* we don't.
   I trust Harry, *for* I know him well. (*For* means "because.")

The two sentences joined together this way make one compound sentence with two independent clauses (that is, clauses that could stand alone as sentences). We use a comma between the two clauses to help the reader see an important dividing point, but a comma alone is not enough to join two sentences or independent clauses. We would make an error known as a comma splice unless we also had one of these joining words (called *conjunctions*): *and, but, or, nor, for, so* and *yet.* It pays to memorize these seven powerful words. They are the only words that can join clauses of equal rank (importance) without a semicolon.
   A semicolon is a cross between a comma and a period; it is stronger than a

comma but weaker than a period. A period separates sentences; a semicolon joins them. The semicolon may be used in a compound sentence in place of a joining word (conjunction) as in this example:

I know Harry well; I trust him.

The semicolon is particularly effective for contrasting or opposing ideas:

I'll go to my church; you go to yours.
Ask not what your country can do for you; ask what you can do for your country.

A compound sentence still needs a semicolon between the clauses when words like *however, nevertheless, moreover, then,* and *therefore* are used.

I know Harry well; *however,* I don't trust him.
I know Harry well; *therefore,* I trust him.
I don't know Harry very well; *nevertheless,* I trust him.

These words are adverbs, not joining words. Unlike true joining words, they can be moved around in the clause, as in these examples:

I know Harry well; I don't trust him, *however.*
I know Harry well; I *therefore* trust him.

The semicolon stays between the two clauses no matter where we put *however* and *therefore*. And if we use only a comma between clauses, we make the error known as a comma splice (splicing two sentences together with a comma).

Comma Splice: We don't carry Western jeans, however, we have the Levi brand.
Corrected: We don't carry Western jeans; however, we have the Levi brand.

For more information, see the handbook section on "Fused and Comma-Spliced Sentences."

Choose the joining word that suits your purpose best. The semicolon is best for strong, sharp contrast. The conjunction *and* is best when the second clause adds information to the first clause. The conjunction *but* shows contrast or takes something away. *Or* and *nor* express choices or lack of choices. The conjunction *for* means "because," so use it only when the second clause causes the first one (for example, "I can't buy a ticket, *for* I don't have the money"). The conjunction *so* means "therefore." It shows that the first clause causes the second one (for example, "I don't have the money, *so* I can't buy a ticket"). The conjunction *yet* shows a contrast we would not ordinarily expect (for example, "They don't have much money, *yet* they give generously to others").

Compound sentences may contain more than two independent clauses, like this one:

Leaders may come, and leaders may go, but the nation stays the same.

DO NOT WRITE IN THIS BOOK

Sentence Combining 10.0
Writing Better Compound Sentences

Beginning writers often overuse the word *and,* especially in joining compound sentences. Often one of the other joining words shows a clearer logical relationship. The semicolon, too, may be a more effective choice, especially when a sharp contrast of opposites is desired.

Combine the sentences below into compound sentences without using *and.* Use a semicolon if that would be best, or choose the most logical joining word from this group of conjunctions: *but, or, nor, for, so, yet.* Remember to use a comma along with the conjunction (joining word) between the two halves of a compound sentence.

Example: You have your opinion. I have mine.
Combined: You have your opinion; I have mine. (Sharp contrast shown.)

1 Last month the coal miners went on strike. This month it's the steel workers.

_____

_____

2 The steel producers and the unions have been bargaining for a week. They still have not come to an agreement.

_____

_____

3 The producers and the union members are all getting worried. Everyone is losing money while the strike lasts.

_____

_____

4 Workers are losing wages. They are worried. Producers are losing profits. They are worried, too.

_____

_____

5 The producers offered a wage increase. The union members want a better pension plan in addition.

_____

_____

6 The producers asked the President to stop the strike. The President does not want to interfere if he can help it.

_____

_____

7 However, the President is concerned. The wage settlement could have a considerable effect on inflation.

_____

_____

8 According to the last public opinion poll, the people do not sympathize with the producers. They do not sympathize with the unions.

_____

_____

9 The steel producers can win. The union can win. It doesn't matter to the public as long as the strike gets settled.

_____

_____

10 Strikes will never be popular with the general public. Strikes seem to be here to stay.

Controlled Composition 10.1
Combining to Make Compound Sentences

In your own notebook, rewrite the following passage. Combine sentences 2 and 3, sentences 4 and 5, sentences 6 and 7, sentences 8 and 9, sentences 11 and 12, and sentences 13 and 14. Be sure to use a comma with the conjunctions *and, but, or, nor, for, so,* and *yet;* also be sure to choose the one that makes the best sense. You may use a semicolon (;) instead of a conjunction when the ideas are closely related or show sharp contrast.

Put a box around each of your changes, proofread, and have your instructor check your paper against the answer key. When you join sentences 2 and 3, they will look like one of these:

In right-handed persons, the left brain is usually dominant $\boxed{;\ \textbf{in}}$ left-handed persons, the right brain usually is.

In right-handed persons, the left brain is usually dominant $\boxed{,\ \textbf{but}}$ in left-handed persons, the right brain usually is.

How the Two Halves of the Brain Work

(1) Recent brain research shows that the left and right halves of the brain each play a different part in learning. (2) In right-handed persons, the left brain is usually dominant. (3) In left-handed persons, the right brain usually is.

(4) The brain functions are too complex to explain fully here. (5) However, some simplified explanations can be given, if we realize that exceptions exist. (6) Generally in right-handed persons, the left brain controls math and language learning, logic, and a sense of time. (7) It observes and analyzes details. (8) The right brain controls intuition, imagination, concepts of space, images, drawing, and dancing. (9) It responds to whole patterns, shapes, rhythm, sounds, and colors.

(10) The most effective learning involves both halves of the brain. (11) The left brain thinks in details and sequences. (12) The right brain thinks with insight

and puts the details into meaningful wholes. (13) The left brain reasons logically. (14) The right brain responds emotionally. (15) Creative thinking probably begins in the right brain with some vision, idea, or insight into a problem. (16) Then the left brain works out the details that turn the vision or dream into a real product such as a song, a composition, a painting, a poem, or a new application of science.

Controlled Composition 10.2

Rewrite the passage below in your notebook, making the following changes. Join the following pairs of sentences with semicolons: 6 and 7, 8 and 9, 10 and 11, 12 and 13, 14 and 15. Join the following pairs of sentences with the joining words *but, so,* or *for,* whichever is most logical: 16 and 17, 18 and 19, 20 and 21.

Put a box around each of your changes, proofread, and have your instructor check your paper against the answer key. Your combination of sentences 6 and 7 will look like this:

The superior person wants to have good character $\boxed{; \textbf{the}}$ inferior person wants to have a high place in society.

Confucius and the Superior Person

(1) Confucius (pronounced "con-FEW-shuss") was a Chinese wise man. (2) His writings taught people how to get along with each other in satisfying ways. (3) To Confucius, people were superior or inferior depending upon their thoughts and behavior toward others. (4) This is how he explained it.

(5) The superior person feels related to all humanity, not just his or her own countrymen or social class. (6) The superior person wants to have good character. (7) The inferior person wants to have a high place in society. (8) The superior person wants justice. (9) The inferior person wants favors. (10) The superior person asks a lot of himself. (11) The inferior person asks a lot from others. (12) The superior person thinks of what is right. (13) The inferior person thinks of what will pay. (14) The superior person wants knowledge. (15) The inferior person wants to be known.

(16) The superior person is not concerned about not being given a place. (17) He is concerned about making himself fit for one. (18) Doing good work is more important to him than getting praises or prizes for it. (19) He always does the best work he can. (20) He doesn't brag. (21) He knows his deeds should be greater than his words. (22) He always follows this rule: do not do unto others what you would not have them do unto you.

Creating

10.3 Compare and contrast two products you might buy, such as two cars, two houses, two household cleaning products, two brands of clothing, and so on. Use compound sentences at least two or three times in your paragraph to make the contrast especially clear.

10.4 Compare and contrast the personalities of two pets, two children, or two employers you have known. Use compound sentences to make the contrast sharp (at least two or three compound sentences in your paper).

10.5 Think about this quotation: "God made the country, and man made the town." The contrast is clear because it is made in a compound sentence. Write a paragraph contrasting town living with country living, using at least two or three compound sentences in your paper.

LESSON
11

Subordinating with Adverbial Clauses

Notice how the following two sentences are combined in several ways:

We eat dinner. Then your friends can come over.
After we eat dinner, your friends can come over.
Until we eat, your friends can't come over.
When we have eaten, your friends can come over.

Strangely enough, *We eat dinner* is a complete sentence, but the words *after we eat dinner* are not a complete sentence. When we hear them, we expect more to come.

We can take a basic sentence like *We eat dinner* and turn it into an adverbial clause, or dependent clause, with joining words (conjunctions) like these:

after we eat	*if* we eat	*when* we eat
although we eat	*in order that* we eat	*whenever* we eat
as we eat	*since* we eat	*where* we eat
as if we eat	*so that* we eat	*wherever* we eat
because we eat	*though* we eat	*whether* we eat
before we eat	*unless* we eat	*while* we eat

Now we have subordinated the clause, or turned it into a modifier telling when, where, why, and so on. Then we must attach it to another sentence, which is called the *main clause* or *independent clause*. We can attach it at the beginning, at the end, or even in the middle of the main clause. If we put it at the end, no punctuation is needed because no confusion can result:

Your friends can come over *after we eat.*

When we put adverbial clauses at the beginning, however, our readers can get confused. For example, they might start to read the sentence below "when you have eaten your friends"—and think you are a cannibal!

When you have eaten your friends can come over.

To signal the reader that the modifier has ended and the main clause is starting, we put a comma after *eaten* in that sentence. Then the reader can't get confused. We do the same for any adverbial clause placed before a main clause. We can also help our reader by using commas to enclose an adverbial clause inserted in the middle of a main clause. See how these two sentences are combined:

Americans often eat badly. They eat a lot of food.
Americans, although they eat a lot of food, often eat badly.

Two commas are needed to mark both ends of the adverbial clause here because it interrupts the thought of the main clause.

Sometimes two sentences can be combined by subordinating either one of them, as in this example:

Although I like Angela, I don't always agree with her.
Although I don't always agree with her, I like Angela.

Writers should always put the most important idea in the main clause and the less important idea in the subordinate clause (modifying clause). The first sentence about Angela stresses not agreeing with her. The second one stresses liking her. Remember that adverbial joining words cripple a clause and make it dependent, so be sure you subordinate the less important clause.

We must never treat a dependent clause as if it were a sentence. That would create the kind of sentence fragment underlined in the examples below:

I trust Harry. Because I know him well.

I need a car. Although I can't afford it.

Such fragments can easily be prevented by attaching them to the main clause, either at the end or at the beginning:

I trust Harry because I know him well. (no comma needed)
Although I can't afford it, I need a car. (comma needed)

Adverbial clauses can be shortened to phrases by leaving out the subject and verb, like this:

Clauses	**Phrases**
After (we eat) dinner	After dinner
Before (you take) your test	Before your test
Whenever (it is) possible	Whenever possible
If (this is) agreeable to you	If agreeable to you

Like adverbial clauses, adverbial phrases are modifiers that tell when, where, why, how, or under what conditions the main action takes place. Punctuate adverbial phrases in the same way you do clauses. A comma is particularly important after long introductory adverbial phrases like these:

Whenever possible without surrender, be on good terms with all men.

Although seemingly unimportant at the time, small mistakes add up.

Sentence Combining 11.0
Making Adverbial Clauses

Combine the following paired sentences into sentences with adverbial clauses, using the joining word suggested in parentheses (like this). Use the sentence with the more important idea as your main clause, and turn the less important one into a dependent clause, or modifier, with the joining word. You may change the clauses around and put either one at the beginning. If you put the dependent clause first, remember to follow it with a comma.

Example: (whenever) I leave the house. I lock the door.
Combined: Whenever I leave the house, I lock the door. (comma needed)
Or: I lock the door whenever I leave the house. (no comma)
It would not be logical to say, "Whenever I lock the door, I leave the house."

1 (when) You may take your first lesson.
You have completed your application form and paid your fee.

_____

_____

2 (until) An accident occurred at the nuclear plant.
All the citizens felt safe.

_____

_____

3 (where) I left my glasses.
I can never seem to remember.   DO NOT WRITE IN THIS BOOK

_____

_____

4 (while) The children were setting the table.
Dad started the campfire.

_____

_____

5 (unless) You may not get tickets.
You make reservations well ahead of time.

_____

_____

6 (because) A defect has been discovered in the brake system.
The Aghast Motor Company is recalling its new model cars.

_____

_____

7 (if) The paint is not dry.
Let it stand another ten minutes.

_____

_____

8 (although) Jackie's points were good ones.
Don's arguments were more convincing.

_____

_____

9 (in order that) We must repair the track.
We can hold a track meet here in May.

_____

_____

10 (after) The nominating committee submits three names.
The officers are elected by the members at the April meeting.

_____

_____

Rearrange the following sentences by inserting the adverbial clause at a suitable place inside the main clause. Enclose the inserted clause with commas, as in the example below. The adverbial clauses are underlined to help you see them as a unit that can be moved around in the larger sentence.

Example: If it works out as planned, the dance should be a great success.

The dance, if it works out as planned, should be a great success.

11 Even if his life depended on it, Leroy could never keep his checkbook in balance.

_____

_____

12 Whether or not they win the tournament, the team members have a right to feel proud.

_____

_____

13 It is always wise to get permission <u>before you give someone's name as a reference.</u>

_____

_____

14 Women artists are rarely discussed in art history books <u>although many were famous in their own lifetimes.</u>

_____

_____

15 The Beatles attracted new fans and admirers <u>wherever they went.</u>

_____

_____

Controlled Composition 11.1
Practice Subordinating with Adverbial Clauses

Rewrite the following passage in your notebook, making the following changes. In sentence 1, begin with *although* and remove *yet*. In sentence 2, begin with *because* and remove *so*. In sentence 4, begin with *although* and remove *but*. In sentence 9, use *because* in place of *for* (watch the logic here; get *because* in the right place). In sentence 10, begin with *if* and remove *so*.

Put a box around each of your changes, proofread to be sure the whole passage makes sense, and have your instructor check your paper against the answer key. Your first sentence, when changed, will look like this:

Although | Americans eat more food than most other nationalities, many of us are starving our bodies and minds.

Can Foods Affect Our Moods?

(1) Americans eat more food than most other nationalities, yet many of us are starving our bodies and minds. (2) We eat "junk foods" like soft drinks, candy, and potato chips, so we are getting lots of calories but not enough minerals and vitamins. (3) Many of our favorite snacks are salty foods, but eating too much salt can lead to tension, headaches, high blood pressure, and heart disease. (4) We love hot dogs and cold cuts, but these favorites contain food colorings and preservatives that can contribute to such health problems as mental depression, hyperactivity, and learning disabilities. (5) We need B-complex vitamins to deal with stress, yet we often eat white bread, white rice, and spaghetti products with all the vitamins taken out. (6) Sugar not only adds weight and decays teeth, but also can cause mental depression, tiredness, hyperactivity, and learning problems. (7) Even if we avoid candy, hidden sugar abounds in many products such as catsup and canned fruits. (8) Coffee and tea, in excess, can also lead to nervousness, depression, and tiredness after the temporary "lift" wears off. (9) Today we need more vitamin C than ever, for it helps fight infections and pollutants from our air and water. (10) We want to be mentally alert and physically strong, so we should eat only nutritious foods. (11) Bad diets can make us tired, depressed, and unable to think clearly. (12) They can spoil our chances for happiness.

Controlled Composition 11.2

Rewrite the passage below in your notebook, making the following changes and punctuating as needed. In sentences 1 and 4, begin with *although* and remove *but*. In sentence 5, begin with *because* and remove *so*. At the END of sentence 6, add *since liquid removers sometimes dissolve nylon brushes.* At the BEGINNING of sentence 9, add *before you apply the mixture.* At the END of sentence 11, add *until all the old paint has been removed.*

Put a box around each of your changes, proofread, and have your instructor check your paper against the answer key. Your first sentence, when changed, will look like this:

Although refinishing old furniture takes time and effort, it can be very satisfying.

Refinishing Old Furniture
(Adapted from *The Feminine Fix-It Handbook,* by Kay B. Ward)

(1) Refinishing old furniture takes time and effort, but it can be very satisfying. (2) If the old surface is good, just wash it to remove old wax and sand it to make

it slightly rough before repainting. (3) If the old surface is bad, you must remove it. (4) Liquid paint remover made for professional furniture finishers is strong and inexpensive, but it catches fire more easily than the paint store kind. (5) It can burn skin and ruin clothes, so it must be used with care. (6) Use inexpensive bristle paintbrushes. (7) Combine the paint remover half and half with paint thinner. (8) If you get any on your skin, remove it at once with paint thinner. (9) Spread newspapers around the work area, and take off all removable handles and decorations. (10) When the remover has been on for about twenty minutes, the paint should be soft enough to scrape off with a putty knife. (11) Repeat if necessary.

From *The Feminine Fix-It Handbook* by Kay B. Ward. Copyright © 1972 by Kay B. Ward. Used by Permission of Grosset & Dunlap, Inc.

Challenge: Can you find four adverbial clauses in the above passage other than the ones you added or changed?

Creating

11.3 Plan a vacation trip, using adverbial clauses similar to these: *if we can get the time off work, when we arrive, in order to be sure we haven't forgotten anything, after it's all over.* Remember the comma to signal the end of the adverbial clause and the beginning of the main clause.

11.4 Plan a future career. Begin several sentences with adverbial clauses starting with such words as *when, if, where, because, although, before, as, since, unless,* and so on.

11.5 Explain how to do a repair job. Begin or end several sentences with adverbial clauses, using commas where needed. These clauses might begin with *if, when, where, because, until, since, before, as, while, although, unless, so that,* and so on. (See the complete list on the first page of this lesson.)

LESSON
12

Subordinating with Adjective Clauses

In Lesson 11, we combined two sentences by making one of them into an adverbial clause. Another way to combine sentences is to turn one of them into a dependent clause that works like an adjective, describing some noun in the main clause. These adjective clauses answer the questions "Which one?" or "What kind?" about the word they modify. They begin with *who, whom, whose* (for people); *which* (for things): or *that* (for either persons or things).

Here's how this kind of combination works:

1. **Two Sentences:**   He is a man. *He* does good work.
   Combined: He is a man *who* does good work.
   (When the sentences are combined, the second *he* is replaced by *who*.)

2. **Two Sentences:**   Hawaii is a place. Everyone wants to see *it*.
   Combined: Hawaii is a place *that* everyone wants to see.
   (*It* is replaced by *that*.)

3. **Two Sentences:**   You returned the pants for credit. We received *them*.
   Combined: We received the pants *which* you returned for credit.
   (*Them* is replaced by *which*.)

4. **Two Sentences:**   Mark Twain is a humorist. I admire *his* work.
   Combined: Mark Twain is a humorist *whose* work I admire.
   (*His* is replaced by *whose*.)

5. **Two Sentences:**   He was my last employer. I worked for *him.*
   Combined: He was the last employer for *whom* I worked.
                        (*Him* is replaced by *whom.*)

None of the examples above require commas. But some adjective clauses require two commas to enclose them. When the person or thing is already fully identified, the adjective clause isn't necessary to tell "which one." It gives extra information, so it needs two extra commas. Here are some examples:

1. Mark Twain, who wrote *Huckleberry Finn,* is America's most famous humorist. (His name fully identifies him, so the clause is extra.)
2. Twain's last book, which was published after his death, made fun of certain religious customs. (There can be only one last book, so the adjective clause is extra information, requiring extra commas.)

The above examples can be considered as sentence-combining that inserts one sentence inside the other, like this:

1. **Two Sentences:**   Mark Twain is America's most famous humorist. He wrote *Huckleberry Finn.*
   Combined: Mark Twain, who wrote *Huckleberry Finn,* is America's most famous humorist.
2. **Two Sentences:**   My boss really knows the business. He started at the bottom.
   Combined: My boss, who started at the bottom, really knows the business.

Sometimes the introductory words *who, whom, which,* and *that* are left out and just understood to be there. The words in parentheses below could be left out without affecting the meaning:

The waitress (whom) I like best is getting married.
The car (that) Jim is driving has faulty brakes.
You can spend all the money (which) you earn.

Like adverbial clauses, adjective clauses are not complete sentences. If we punctuate an adjective clause like a sentence, we make a fragment like those underlined below.

Wally wanted to sit near the front. Which was fine with me.

Diane is a girl with talent. Who should really go far.

These fragments can easily be corrected by attaching them to the preceding sentences, like this:

Wally wanted to sit near the front, which was fine with me.
Diane is a girl with talent who should really go far.

For more information about *who* and *whom*, see Section 10 of the Handbook.

Sentence Combining 12.0
Making Adjective Clauses

Combine the following pairs of sentences into sentences with adjective clauses, using the joining word suggested in parentheses. Punctuate as shown in Lesson 12. Use the most important idea for your main clause and the less important one for your adjective clause (modifier). You will have to drop some words because they are replaced by the joining word, as *it* is replaced by *that* in this example:

Two Sentences: Apple pie is a dessert. Everyone likes *it*.
Combined: Apple pie is a dessert *that* everyone likes.

1 (which) Liver is wonderful food. Many people dislike it.

_____

_____

2 (which) Here are the magazines. You ordered them last week.

_____

_____

3 (who) The college attracted good teachers. They love students.

_____

_____

4 (who) I need a tutor. She can help me with my math.

_____

_____

5 (that) A truism is a common saying. Everybody has heard it.

_____

_____

6 (that) Did you know this? Tom is an excellent bridge player.

_____

_____

7 (whose) This award goes to Marilyn. Her sales record was the best this month.

_____

_____

8 (whose) Fred is a writer. His play won a prize last year.

_____

_____

9 (whom) Give this letter to the salesman. It is addressed to him.

_____

_____

10 (whom) Now we will test the sincerity of the senators. We voted for them.

_____

_____

Combine the following pairs of sentences by changing the second one into an adjective clause (beginning with the word in parentheses) and inserting it inside the main clause at a suitable place. Use commas to enclose the inserted clause.

Example: (who) Uncle Ben took me along. He never missed a chance to go fishing.

Combined: Uncle Ben, who never missed a chance to go fishing, took me along.

11 (who) Elvis Presley changed rock 'n' roll history. He died in 1977.

_____

_____

12 (which) The movie got more interesting at the end. It seemed dull at first.

_____

_____

13 (which) The experience of grief is sometimes disabling. Everyone goes through it.

_____

_____

14 (whose) Mark Twain was once a newspaper reporter. His real name was Samuel Clemens.

_____

_____

15 (whom) My parents made sacrifices to send me to college. I will always be grateful to them.

_____

_____

_____

Controlled Composition 12.1
Practice Subordinating with Adjective Clauses

Rewrite the passage below, making the following changes: combine sentences 1 and 2, using *that*. Combine sentences 3 and 4, using *which*. In sentence 5, insert after *boss* the clause *who has better things to do,* enclosing it in commas. Combine sentences 11 and 12, using *who*. Combine sentences 16 and 17, using *whose*.

Put a box around each of your changes, proofread to be sure you have followed directions properly, and have your instructor check your paper against the answer key. Your first sentence, when changed, will look like this:

Most successful people possess certain admirable qualities ⬛that⬛ ⬛you⬛ can imitate.

What Makes a Successful Employee?

(1) Most successful people possess certain admirable qualities. (2) You can imitate these qualities. (3) Most important is the ability to get along with others. (4) This ability includes unselfishness, cooperation, accepting the way others work, and having a sense of humor. (5) Next is responsibility, getting the job done without having the boss standing over you. (6) You should be honest, stealing neither supplies nor time from your employer. (7) You should be self-disciplined, coming on time and working even when you feel "blue." (8) You should be flexible enough to adjust to a new machine or a change in plans, yet conforming enough so that your work fits in with the work of others. (9) Efficiency means not only working fast, but also doing the most important thing first.

(10) Successful people have superior communication skills. (11) They are good speakers. (12) They also know how to listen to others and hear them accurately. (13) They are willing to rewrite their letters and reports until they are very clear and understandable. (14) Above all, they take pride in doing good work. (15) They try to do every task better than they did before, and they do it over if the first attempt doesn't meet their standards. (16) They are valuable employees. (17) Their work is highly regarded. (18) You can be like them.

Controlled Composition 12.2

Rewrite the passage below, making the following changes. Combine sentences 1 and 2, using *who*. Combine sentences 3 and 4, using *which*. Combine sentences 5 and 6, using *who*. Combine sentences 7 and 8, using *that* (be careful to drop the extra word when you combine these two). Combine sentences 9 and 10, using *which*. Combine sentences 13 and 14, using *which*.

In sentence 18, insert after *Lindbergh* the clause *who had all the skill he needed*. Punctuate correctly. In sentence 19, insert after *Hamill* the clause *whose skill was certainly great enough*. Punctuate correctly. Don't take anything out of sentences 18 and 19.

Put a box around each of your changes, proofread to make sure the whole passage makes sense, and have your instructor check it against the answer key. Your first two sentences, when combined, will look like this:

(1–2) Charles Lindbergh was a famous pilot who flew alone across the Atlantic in 1927.

Lindbergh and Hamill

(1) Charles Lindbergh was a famous pilot. (2) He flew alone across the Atlantic in 1927. (3) This was a great accomplishment. (4) No one had ever done it before. (5) Dorothy Hamill was a famous figure skater. (6) She won the Olympic skating championship. (7) Both Lindbergh and Hamill had special talent. (8) Other people don't have talent to the same degree. (9) Lindbergh also had many years of flying experience behind him. (10) This experience helped him to make judgments about weather conditions and about what his plane could do. (11) Hamill had practiced hundreds of hours.

(12) But both of them had something more than talent and experience. (13) They had a winning attitude. (14) This attitude made it possible for them to keep going even when others were saying it couldn't be done. (15) They both believed in themselves and said, "I know I can do it." (16) Of course, just having a good attitude isn't enough to make winners of us. (17) But having a bad attitude can always make losers of us. (18) Imagine what would have happened if Charles Lindbergh had said, "It's never been done before; it can't be done." (19) Imagine what would have happened if Dorothy Hamill had said, "I don't think I'm good enough to be a champion." (20) Then this passage might be written about two other less talented, but more courageous, people.

Creating

12.3   Think about this quotation: "A man who doesn't have time for little things can't be trusted with big things." Write about the importance of little things. Use some clauses beginning with *who, which,* and *that* in at least three sentences, and underline those clauses.

12.4   Write about a person who has influenced you or a person whom you admire or a person whose life has inspired you. In your paper, use some clauses beginning with at least three of these words: *who, whom, whose, which, that.* Underline all the adjective clauses you use.

LESSON
13

Using Appositives and Interrupters

Notice the similarity between these two sentences. Which sounds better to you?

1. My boss, who is a patient man, explained again.
2. My boss, a patient man, explained again.

Both are combinations of two sentence ideas (1) my boss is a patient man, and (2) he explained again. But the second one is simpler, saying the same thing in fewer words. Notice a similar pattern in the following sentences:

1. The football players, who were happy and excited, headed home.
2. The football players, happy and excited, headed home.

You will probably recognize the sentence pattern in both of the number one sentences; they contain adjective clauses. The number two sentences contain appositives—first an appositive noun, then an appositive adjective. The word *appositive* means "next to"; it is a word or phrase that renames or describes the noun next to it.

The appositives above are interrupters. They interrupt the main clause, and two commas are needed to set them apart from the main clause. But interrupters can also begin or end a sentence. When we want to emphasize a modifier we can put it at the beginning of the sentence like this:

1. Happy and excited, the team headed home.
2. Disappointed but patient, my boss explained again.

Usually, however, the modifier word groups are placed in less emphatic positions because the writer wants to stress the idea in the main clause.

Another kind of interrupter uses an -ing word or a word group beginning with an -ing word. Here are some examples:

1. The team, glowing with victory, headed home.
2. The boss, sighing patiently, explained again.

Although interrupters are usually enclosed with commas, they can also be enclosed with parentheses (like this) or with dashes—like this—used in pairs. Parentheses are used for adding less important details, and dashes are used for emphasis. Here are some examples:

1. The new girl—a sensation in a bikini—had all eyes upon her.
2. Wendy says (nothing she says can be believed) that the new girl once modeled professionally.

When the interrupter contains a series inside it that requires commas, we enclose the interrupter with dashes to avoid confusion about where the interrupter begins and ends. Here is an example:

The beauty of ordinary things—a sunset, a flower, a baby—can be appreciated freshly again and again.

You will learn more about punctuating items in a series in Lesson 15.

Sometimes constructions that look like interrupters are needed to identify fully the person or thing they describe. In that case, they are not interrupters, and no commas are used. A good test for these is that they cannot be moved around in the sentence; they are fixed to the word they modify. Here are some examples:

1. Have you see a child wearing a red shirt and blue jeans?
2. A person deprived of affection is like a person starved for food.

Appositives are not sentences by themselves. They must be imbedded in a sentence or attached to one. If we punctuate them with capitals and periods, we create fragments like those underlined below.

1. My dad is a great Scrabble player. One who can win every time.

2. We need a good secretary. A person who can take shorthand.
3. Carl is a good friend. The best friend I ever had.

These fragments can be corrected by attaching them to the preceding sentences, like this:

1. My dad is a great Scrabble player, one who can win every time.
2. We need a good secretary, a person who can take shorthand.
3. Carl is a good friend—the best friend I ever had.

For more information about commas, parentheses, and dashes, see the Handbook, Sections 16 and 20.

Sentence Combining 13.0
Making Appositives and Interrupters

A. **Combine the sentences below by making the second one into an appositive or interrupter and inserting it into the first sentence near the noun it describes or renames. Here the nouns are fully identified, so you will need extra commas to enclose the extra information in the appositive.**

Example: Babe Ruth made a great many strikeouts. He was the famous home-run hitter.
Combined: Babe Ruth, the famous home-run hitter, made a great many strikeouts.

1 Mary Jo Mulberry is now an actress. She is a former Miss America.

_____

_____

2 Tonight's speaker is Ralph Radar. He is an outspoken opponent of nuclear power.

_____

_____

3 America's favorite television show has been playing for thirty years. It is "I Love Lucy."

_____

_____

4 Professor Dabbs will teach creative writing this spring. He is a talented writer and photographer.

_____

_____

5 Many people have been helped by Alcoholics Anonymous. It is an organization for problem drinkers.

_____

_____

6 The first step is the hardest. It is admitting that you are an alcoholic.

_____

_____

7 The big buck bounded across the clearing. He was proud and graceful.

_____

_____

8 The hunters returned to camp. They were grumbling about their bad luck.

_____

_____

9 At midnight the wives went to bed. They were bored by their husbands' often-repeated stories.

_____

_____

10 Some thieves robbed several homes in the neighborhood. They were gaining entrance through sliding glass doors.

_____

_____

B. Appositives needed to identify a noun do not use commas. Insert the words in parentheses into the sentences below as appositives without commas.

Example: (consumers) We must read labels carefully.
Combined: We consumers must read labels carefully.

11 (Ben) My brother is a pilot.   DO NOT WRITE IN THIS BOOK

_____

_____

12 (_Coming Home_) Have you seen the movie?

_____

_____

13 (_Bless Me, Ultima_) The book is about a woman with special powers.

_____

_____

14 (women) Your threats won't frighten us.

_____

_____

15 (aspirin) The common drug has many different uses.

_____

_____

C. **Insert the words in parentheses into the sentences below, using dashes to enclose the interrupter. (If the second dash would come at the end of the sentence, only a period is needed there.)**

Example: (coffee, tea, and chocolate) Our favorite drinks may all be harmful in some ways.
Combined: Our favorite drinks—coffee, tea, and chocolate—may all be harmful in some ways.

16 (cinnamon, ginger, and cloves) Add the necessary spices before you sift the flour.

_____

_____

17 (honor, truthfulness, cleanliness) He had all the Boy Scout virtues, but he never seemed smug.

_____

_____

18 (to live or to win) When faced with this bitter choice, Vince Lombardi chose to win.

_____

_____

19 (and I'm sorry to admit this) The class average was only 45.

_____

_____

20 (to work and to love) Freud said there are two things that every human being can do.

_____

_____

> **D. Correct the appositive fragments below by attaching them to the previous sentence.**
>
> **Example:** I'd like a good job. One that pays well.
> **Corrected:** I'd like a good job, one that pays well.

21 Dr. Allison is a good chemistry teacher. One who really knows how to explain things.

_____

_____

22 My mom is a wonderful person. Someone I can always count on.

_____

_____

23 This town needs a councilman like Higgins. A decent family man.

_____

_____

24 We bought a new car. One with power brakes and steering.

_____

_____

25 I'm interested in office work. Either bookkeeping or typing.

Controlled Composition 13.1
Practice with Appositives and Interrupters

Rewrite the passage below, making the following changes. In sentence 2, add the following interrupters, using commas where needed: *forcing forth from Binta's strong young body,* and *flecked and slippery with her blood.* In sentence 3, insert these names after *midwives: old Nyo Boto and the baby's grandmother Yaisa.* In sentence 6, insert these adjectives describing the thin blue smoke: *pungent and pleasant.* In sentence 8, add *hastening from their beds of bamboo cane and cured hides.* In sentence 9, add *beaming and excited* to describe the new father. Use commas where needed.

Put a box around each of your changes, proofread, and have your instructor check your paper against the answer key. More than one combination may be possible, so choose the one that sounds best to you. Sentence 2, when changed, will look like this:

| **Forcing forth from Binta's strong young body,** | he was as black as his |

mother was, | **flecked and slippery with her blood,** | and he was bawling.

The Birth of Kunta Kinte
(Adapted from *Roots,* by Alex Haley)

(1) Early in the spring of 1750, in the village of Juffure, West Africa, a manchild was born to Omoro and Binta Kinte. (2) He was as black as his mother was, and he was bawling. (3) The two wrinkled midwives saw that it was a boy and laughed with joy. (4) There was the prideful knowledge that the name of Kinte would thus be perpetuated.

(5) The traditional breakfast of porridge was cooked in earthen pots over a fire built among three rocks. (6) The thin blue smoke went curling up over the small dusty village of round mud huts. (7) The wailing of Kajali Demba, the village alimamo, began, calling men to the first of five daily prayers. (8) The men of the village filed briskly to the praying place, where the alimamo led the worship: "God is great! There is only one God!" (9) As the men were returning

toward their homes for breakfast, Omoro rushed among them to tell them of his firstborn son.

Excerpted from *Roots* by Alex Haley. Copyright © 1976 by Alex Haley. Reprinted by permission of Doubleday & Company, Inc.

Controlled Composition 13.2

Rewrite the passage below, making the following changes and punctuating wherever necessary. In sentence 1, insert the interrupter *for no apparent reason* after the word *when*. In sentence 4, insert after *doctors* the appositive *Dr. Swoboda of Vienna and Dr. Fleiss of Berlin*. In sentence 5, insert after *doctors* the interrupter *working separately and without any knowledge of each other's research*. In sentence 8, insert after *upswing* the interrupter *or the other way around*. In sentence 9, insert after *cycle* the appositive *the 33-day intellectual rhythm*. Also in sentence 9, insert after *Teltscher* the appositive *an Austrian math professor*.

Put a box around each of your changes, proofread, and have your instructor check your paper against the answer key. Your first sentence, when changed, will look like this:

All of us have days when $\boxed{\textbf{, for no apparent reason,}}$ the bottom drops out.

Biorhythm: Good Days and Bad Days

(1) All of us have days when the bottom drops out. (2) We feel like klutzes, or emotional basket cases, or woodenheads. (3) But on other days we feel we are "hitting on all cylinders," as we breeze through difficult tasks or wrap up the day's work an hour early. (4) Early in the twentieth century two European doctors offered a theory called "biorhythm" to explain our good days and bad days. (5) These doctors had both discovered that human beings have 23-day physical cycles and 28-day emotional cycles that begin at birth and continue throughout our lives. (6) During the upswing phase of the cycle, we can perform best. (7) During the downswing phase, our bodies are resting and regaining strength. (8) When we switch over from downswing to upswing, we have "critical days" when we are more likely to get sick or use poor judgment. (9) A third cycle was discovered by Alfred Teltscher during the 1920s. (10) He found that his students memorized better on certain days, and such "good days" went in 33-day cycles. (11) Biorhythm theory has been used by bus companies to reduce accidents, by surgeons to help patients, and by coaches to improve athletes' performances.

Creating

13.3   Write a brief story (it can be a funny one) about people you work with, classmates, or members of a group you belong to, using appositives to explain who each person in the group is or what he or she is like. Underline the appositives, and use commas where necessary.

13.4   Write a letter to a distant friend, inviting him or her to meet some friends you now have. Use appositives to explain more about the persons he or she will meet. Underline the appositives; use commas where needed.

14

Getting Rid of the Deadwood

Which of these sentences is easier to read?

1. A penny that is saved is equal to a penny that is earned.
2. A penny saved is a penny earned.

Both sentences say the same thing, but the first one uses many unnecessary words. Wasted words are deadwood; they make writing hard to read. Many students "pad" their writing by using more words than they need to express a simple idea they haven't thought much about. A better way to get length in an assigned paper is to give more details or a more complete explanation or several ways of looking at a problem. That shows better thinking, and teachers like good thinking better than a lot of words that say nothing.

Efficient businesspersons dislike padded writing, too. Reading wasted words takes time, and time costs money. Here are some ways to cut out wasted words:

Padded: The letter that you sent to us on July 9 has been received, and we will do our utmost to see that you obtain all of the items that you ordered.

Better: Your letter of July 9 has been received, and we will do our best to send you all the items you ordered.

Best: We received your July 9 letter and will send you everything you ordered.

Often, modifying phrases can be reduced to a single word placed before the noun. Here are some examples (note that compound words joined with a hyphen, like *front-loading,* are considered one word).

A customer of great importance = an important customer.
A machine loading from the front = a front-loading machine.
A worker with a satisfactory record = a satisfactory worker.
A chair built to last a long time = a sturdily built chair.

Adverbial modifiers can also be shortened, as in these examples:

Worked in a hard and steady manner = worked hard and steadily.
Drove in a way that was reckless = drove recklessly.

Some expressions contain an unnecessary repetition of ideas, called *redundancy.* Here are some examples of redundant expressions:

The modern world of today . . .	Say *modern world* or *world of today,* not both.
Final conclusion . . .	A conclusion is always final, so *final* is unnecessary.
Proceed onward . . .	Can you proceed any other way?
An individual person . . .	Either *individual* or *person* is enough.

Sometimes, too, writers use unnecessarily complicated verbs, as in the following examples:

Wordy: His record of employment with us *has always been* satisfactory.
Better: His employment record with us *is* satisfactory.
Wordy: His manner *might be said* to look insincere.
Better: His manner *seems* insincere.

Sentence Practice 14.0
Reducing Wordiness in Sentences

Change the wordy phrases below to say the same thing in fewer words.

Example: A letter with a lot of unnecessary words
Reduced: A wordy letter

1 A car with a lot of power

2 Working at a fast pace

3 A face that looks familiar

4 An actor who is known to everyone

5 Rapid and speedy service

6 A print that is made of many colors

7 A true fact

8 We are in receipt of your letter.

9 Your order has been shipped under separate cover as of the 19th of June.

10 The person who has been elected to serve as your representative can be found at the Charlton Hotel for the greater part of the day on Thursday.

Controlled Composition 14.1
Practice Getting Rid of the Deadwood

Rewrite the passage below, changing the underlined phrases and clauses to give the same information in fewer words. Use the smallest number of words that will still carry the same meaning. Put a box around each of your changes, proofread, and have your instructor compare your paper to the answer key. Your changes may not be exactly the same, but they should be an improvement over the original passage. Sentence 2, when changed, will look like this:

But the $\boxed{\text{Jabberbox}}$ uses words to block communication.

The Jabberbox

For most people, words are a means of communicating with others. But the person whom we might call the Jabberbox uses words to block communication. He hides behind a smoke screen of words that are not necessary. Not only does he get more attention while everyone is trying to figure out what it is that he is saying, but he also keeps others from finding out what he is really like. By discussing only subjects that are trivial or commonplace, he keeps from revealing his thoughts, opinions, or fears in more important matters.

His business letters are long and boring. He uses big words where plain, simple words would be better. He says, "I am in receipt of your letter" (seven words), instead of "I received your letter" (four words). He says, "Make use of these data" instead of "Use these facts."

Apparently, Jabberbox thinks that he will make a big impression with words that have many syllables and sentences that are complicated. He should learn that unnecessary words are deadwood, and a big word is better only if it has a more precise meaning than a smaller word. If he cuts out the deadwood and cuts down the pretense, people might discover that he has something worthwhile to say.

Controlled Composition 14.2

Rewrite the passage below, changing the underlined phrases and clauses to give the same information in fewer words. Use the smallest number of words that will still carry the same meaning. Put a box around each of your changes, proofread, and have your instructor compare your paper to the answer key. Your changes may not be exactly the same, but they should be an improvement over the original passage. Sentence 2, when changed, will look like this:

They are ⌈lazy⌉ people themselves but expect others to work ⌈hard and steadily.⌉

Deadweights

Deadweights are people who drag others down by not pulling their share of the load. They are people who are lazy themselves but expect others to work at a hard and steady rate. They believe that a person who is really clever can find other people to do his work. But most people get tired of doing more than what they believe to be their fair share, and they dump the deadweights.

Discouragers are deadweights, too. They try to drag others down with negative words and discouraging looks. They can talk in an endless way about how difficult or impossible a goal is for someone else. Those who have never entered a tournament for golf players can tell you why you don't have a chance to win.

Those who have never earned an annual salary of $10,000 a year can tell you why you can't earn $15,000 a year. Those who flunked out of college can tell you all of the many and varied reasons why you can't make it. They are dead-weights. Dump them.

Creating

14.3   Write a paper of about 200 words on any subject. Then cut it down to 150 words that still give all the important information.

14.4   Find a business letter that you think is too long. (It could be an advertising letter you received in the mail.) Cut it down as much as you can without leaving out important information and without making it sound like a telegram.

14.5   Write a telegram of not more than fifteen words to your U.S. senator or representative, giving your opinion on some important bill or issue being debated. Refer to the bill by number.

DO NOT WRITE IN THIS BOOK

LESSON
15

Using Words in a Series

How boring and repetitious language would be if every descriptive word required a separate sentence, like this:

Debra is capable. Debra is efficient. Debra is friendly.

It sounds much better to combine these sentences into one. This creates a series, and we use commas to separate the items in the series:

Debra is capable, efficient, and friendly.

The comma before *and* in a series can be left out, but it is preferred in formal writing. Commas become even more helpful to the reader when each item in the series has more than one word, as in these examples:

1. Government *of the people*, *by the people*, and *for the people* shall not perish from the earth.
2. A modern mother must be a *manager of the family budget*, a *chauffeur for her children*, and an *ever-willing companion for her husband*.

When a series is used, every item should be similar in structure (that is, parallel) to the other items. Lincoln's famous phrases would never be remembered if he had said "government of the people, by the people, and which responds to the people." Here are some other examples:

1. **Awkward:** Peggy stopped writing because of lack of time, and she lost interest.
Parallel: Peggy stopped writing because she lacked the time and she lost interest.
Improved by Eliminating the Series: Peggy stopped writing because she lacked both the time and the interest.

(Because the series in the example above has only two items, no comma is used.)

2. **Awkward:** I like hunting, fishing, and to go skiing.
Parallel: I like hunting, fishing, and skiing.
Also Parallel: I like to hunt, to fish, and to ski.

Notice how pleasing the rhythms are in the following paragraph when it is read aloud. It makes very effective use of two parallel series.

Mass media tactlessly dramatize for the teenager his problems. Television magnifies his pimples; radio calls attention to his bad breath; and magazines warn him not to be deodorantly half safe. They tell him what his best friends would not: to sweeten his breath, to straighten his teeth, to wash away his dandruff, to add weight or lose flab, and to correct his posture. With such friendly advice a teenager is lucky if he can escape feeling defective. (From *Between Parent and Teenager,* by Haim Ginott)

Controlled Composition 15.1
Practice with Items in a Series and Parallelism

Rewrite the passage below in regular paragraph form. Join the following sentences together, beginning each combination with *If*. (You will need a comma at the end of the adverbial clause thus created.) Join sentences 2 and 3; 4 and 5; 6 and 7; 8 and 9; 10 and 11; 12 and 13; 14 and 15.

The passage below shows each series lined up in a column to make it easy for you to see the parallel structure and feel the rhythm of it. Change it to the usual sentence form, using commas where needed. Proofread carefully, reading aloud to hear the rhythms. Then have your instructor check your paper against the key. Sentences 2 and 3, when combined, will look like this:

If we value neatness **, our** teenager will be sloppy **,** his room messy **,** his clothes repulsive **,** and his hair uncombed.

From *Between Parent and Teenager* by Dr. Haim Ginott, Macmillan Co., 1969, Avon paperback.

How Teenagers Bug Their Parents
(Adapted from *Between Parent and Teenager*, by Haim Ginott)

(1) Many teenagers have an inner radar that detects what irritates their parents.
(2) We value neatness. (3) Our teenager will be sloppy
               his room messy
               his clothes repulsive
               and his hair uncombed.
(4) We insist on good manners. (5) He will interrupt conversations
               use profanity
               and belch in company.
(6) We enjoy graceful language and good literature. (7) He will speak slang and read comic books.
(8) We treasure peace. (9) He will quarrel with our neighbors
               tease their dogs
               and bully their children.
(10) We stress physical vigor. (11) He will refuse to exercise.
(12) We are worried about pollution and lung cancer. (13) He will smoke.
(14) We prize good marks and academic standards. (15) He will sink to the bottom of his class.

From *Between Parent and Teenager* by Dr. Haim Ginott, Macmillan Co., 1969, Avon paperback.

Controlled Composition 15.2

Rewrite the passage below in regular paragraph form. It is shown with the items in a series in column form to make it easy for you to see the parallel structure and feel the rhythm of it. Change it to the usual sentence form, using commas where needed. Proofread carefully, reading aloud to hear the rhythms. Then have your instructor check your paper against the answer key. Sentence 1, when changed, will look like this:

Human beings are far more complex | **,** | more intelligent | **,** | and more interesting than rats.

The Human Capabilities
(Adapted from *The Wonderful World Within You*, By Roger Williams)

(1) Human beings are far more complex
               more intelligent
               and more interesting than rats. (2) Many
things human beings can do are completely out of reach of all beasts.

(3) We can read and enjoy literature
        ponder about life and the universe
        absorb the thoughts of past ages
        and develop original ideas.
(4) We can appreciate
        and enjoy art
            music
            sculpture
            and drama.
(5) Our agile minds can enjoy complex games and solve mathematical problems that would be of no interest to a beast. (6) We can look with seeing eyes at all aspects of the physical
        chemical
        biological
        and artistic world around us. (7) Human nutrition
is vastly more interesting than rat nutrition because human nutrition influences all human capabilities.

From *The Wonderful World Within You* by Dr. Roger J. Williams. Copyright © 1977 by Dr. Roger J. Williams. Reprinted by permission of Bantam Books, Inc. All rights reserved.

Creating

15.3 Make a list of the places in your town where people like to go for entertainment. Make another list of good places to eat. Then write a paper giving advice to someone who is new in town, using sentences that mention these places in a series. To keep your sentences readable, don't use a series of more than four items in one sentence. Put some items in another sentence. For example, you may want to group the eating places into fast food places and fine restaurants, using a separate series for each group.

15.4 Write a paragraph that could be part of a letter of application, using the reasons given in the list below, but changing them so that you have two or three sentences with parallel items in a series.

Reasons Why I Want This Job

the pay is good	located near home	opportunity to advance
flexible hours	interesting duties	uses my experience

Here is one way to make a parallel series from the above list:

I'd like this job because it offers good pay, flexible hours, and opportunity to advance.

Here is another possible way:

I'd like this job because the pay is good, the hours are flexible, and the duties are interesting.

You may think of other combinations, but be sure the items in the series are parallel, even if you have to change the wording.

LESSON
16

Using Slang

We all use several levels of language, depending on the situation and the people we are talking to or writing to. Here are five sentences saying the same thing with different levels of language:

1. An incompetent female demolished my automobile. (elevated language)
2. A careless woman driver seriously damaged my car. (standard formal English)
3. Some gal who wasn't looking where she was going totaled out my Chevy. (standard informal English)
4. A dumb dame bashed in my heap. (slang)
5. That there she-critter come a barrelin' outa nowheres an' smack-dab flattened my rig. (nonstandard dialect)

Language will not always fall neatly or rigidly into these classifications. Often a "however, she makes sure they will have a good home."
language, but it can be mixed with nonstandard dialect, informal language, and even occasionally with formal language for a special effect. Most of our writing will be standard formal English (as in a term paper for school) or standard informal (as in a personal letter). But slang is colorful, humorous, and fun. It can liven up a newspaper feature (as in assignment 17.2 about rats), give sparkle to a friendly letter, and add humor to a lighthearted memo to the people you work with.

Notice the difference when the same information is written in standard English and then in slang. The first paragraph below might be written in a paper for school; the second one, in a personal letter.

I am learning something about photography, and I really enjoy it. I got a beautiful camera for my birthday last month. Quite by accident I have taken a few good pictures, enough to keep me interested. But most of my pictures are overexposed. I still don't quite understand how to adjust the light mechanism, but I am slowly making progress. With enough determination and intelligence, I may become a real photographer some day.

I'm getting into photography these days, and I really dig it. I got a camera just for blowing out a few candles last month, and it really is a beaut! I've pulled off a few lucky shots, enough to keep me turned on, but most of my pix are fade-outs. I haven't got the hang of the light gadget yet, but I'm catching on a bit at a time. If I stick with it and get my brain in gear, I may get to be a shutterbug yet.

For other examples of slang, see assignments 17.1, 17.2, and 26.1. You may be using slang without realizing it. Or you may be avoiding it, thinking it is "wrong." It's true that slang is out of place in formal writing (as bathing suits are out of place in a fine restaurant), but it can be very effective in informal writing, and most students can do it very well. Foreign students, however, may need the help of a friend or a tutor in learning to recognize slang.

In Controlled Composition 16.1, you will rewrite a passage changing it from formal language to slang. Listed below are some slang terms that you might use, but don't limit yourself to these. Slang changes rapidly from year to year and place to place; use your own crowd's "slanguage." You may need to change these general definitions, too, to fit your story. (For example, the paragraph on photography changed the words "with enough determination" to "if I just stick with it.")

anxiety—getting uptight, uptightness, hangups
disabled—put out of action
stomach—tummy, belly, gut
tension—jitters, nerves, uptightness, stiffness
tense, nervous—uptight, jittery, all shook up, stiff
imagine—dream up
imagination—something that's all in our minds or all in our heads
happen—turn out, come up
often—lots of times
reject someone—put him down, call him a creep or not cool, dump him
a fear—a worry, a bad notion, a scary notion, a boogeyman
being afraid—being scared, getting shook up, getting the willies
friends—buddies, pals, the gang we run with, cronies, our crowd

people—dudes, folks, guys and gals

clumsy person—klutz, jerk, joker, turkey, lame-brain

ordinary person—a Joe, a John Doe, a Jane Doe

exaggerated—blown up, far out, gone wild

learning—trying our wings, getting the hang of something, getting good at
   something, getting squared away

bad—crummy, lousy, rotten, messed up, dumb

no good—a flop, a mess

let go—put an end to (something), drop (something), let loose of

harsh judgment—put-down

mistake, error—a goof, a boo-boo, messing up (something)

replaced—taken over (by something)

cycle of fear—nonstop worrying, nonstop jitters

confidence—feeling good about ourselves, feeling cool

relax—get rid of hangups, let our hair down, hang loose

make a mistake—muff it, blow it, mess up, goof up

serious—wanting something real bad

notice, observe—keep an eye out for something, keep an eye on the ball

control—keep on top of something

adjust—fix up

inferior—low class, not up to snuff, not up to par

developing—starting out, getting the hang of things, getting the kinks out

accept—take (something) for granted, let it be

success—making it

Sentence Practice 16.0
Recognizing Slang in Sentences

**Find the slang words or expressions in the following sentences. Circle them
or write them on a separate sheet; then check your answers against the
answer key.**

1 The dame that bashed in my car was a rotten driver.

2 The shoplifters are really ripping off the department stores.

3 I cooled the test in my ag class, but I flunked the history final.

4 That junkie has been puffing pot and tripping out on acid until he's scrambled
his brains.

5 That music is really far out; it nearly blows my mind.

6 Don't mess with me or jive me, man, and we'll get along fine.

7 He and his buddies were pretty tight for a while, but they had a falling-out.

8 I goofed a little on the first try, but I really blew it on the next one.

9 She's a stuck-up chick with a lot of high-hat ideas, but she's not making it in college.

10 If a cop stops you for boozing or for running a red light, don't hassle him or you may wind up in the slammer.

Controlled Composition 16.1
Practice Using Slang

Rewrite the following passage entirely, using slang instead of standard English. Use the slang of your own region and your own time, or get some ideas from the slang list in Lesson 16. The instructor's answer key will give you one possible version, but yours will, of course, be somewhat different. Slang is fun, so have a good time with this assignment. One possible way to start would be this:

At bottom, getting uptight is a boogeyman you can't put your finger on. Worry can put us out of action with the tummy-whammies, headsplitters, nerves, and jitters, even if the superbad things we dream up don't have a ghost of a chance of coming up in the real world.

What Causes Anxiety?

Basically, anxiety is a fear without a specific focus. Worry can disable us with stomach upset, headaches, tension, and trembling, even if the terrible things we imagine have very little chance of actually happening.

Often anxiety is based on fear of rejection by other people—a fear greatly exaggerated by the imagination. As an illustration, let's take the example of someone learning to play tennis. When he serves a ball out of the court, he thinks, "What a bad serve." After a few more "bad" serves, he extends the judgment to "I'm a terrible server," then to "I'm a terrible tennis player." Eventually, he thinks that he is no good at sports and, finally, that he is just no good. He begins to fear that no one will want him for a friend. His anxiety makes him tense, and tenseness causes him to make even more mistakes. Only by letting go of the harsh judgments can he relax enough to play well. Then the cycle of fear is replaced by the cycle of confidence.

As a serious learner, he can still notice that the ball went out. He can still adjust his strokes to control the ball better. But he should not judge it as "bad" or judge himself as inferior. He's just developing, and he must accept making errors as part of the growth process.

From "The Fender-Bender," an unpublished story by Kevin Cranford. Reprinted by permission of Kevin Cranford.

Controlled Composition 16.2

Rewrite the following passage entirely, using slang instead of the standard English it is written in. Use the slang of your own region and your own time. Your paper will not be exactly like the suggested version in the instructor's answer key, but it should be highly informal and fun. Here are a few slang definitions that might help you get started:

hot—sizzling; younger sister—kid sis; school—slave camp; radio—boogiebox; hit the bank—warped the bank a good one; stopped—hit the brakes; got out—piled out; tires—skins; bumper jack—fender-bender; drive—get rolling; merchant—swindler; high price—a lot of green; old car—old heap.

The Fender-Bender
(Adapted from a story by Kevin Cranford, college student)

One hot summer morning I was coming over the road from California Hot Springs to Porterville. My younger sister was going to school there and I was taking her down. I was listening dreamily to a terrific song on my radio. As I rounded a turn, I didn't let go of the steering wheel, and as a result I hit a granite bank. I kept going a short distance, then pulled off the road and stopped. I got out and saw that the right fender was bent against the tire, causing it to be cut. I took out my bumper jack and bent the fender back enough so I could drive the car. When I got to Porterville, I bought a new fender from a local merchant who charged a high price, but the old car looks new again.

Creating

16.3   Using slang throughout, write a paper about a day when everything went wrong. Make it sound funny to your reader.

16.4   Using slang throughout, write a paper about a time when you were very nervous.

16.5   Using slang throughout, write a paper about a funny experience you have had with money or with a car.

LESSON
17

Changing Slang to Standard English

Lesson 16 mentioned some informal situations where slang can be used effectively. Once in a while it can be used for a startling or humorous *effect* even in formal writing. The example below uses the slang word *whammy* to give more punch to the statement:

> Minority women experience double discrimination, both as women and as members of minority groups. This double whammy puts most of them at the bottom of the economic ladder.

Generally, however, slang is as out of place in formal writing as blue jeans at a formal dance. Can you find any words in the letter of application below that seem to be out of place?

Dear Sirs:

   I am itching to work for your company. I have had considerable training in this type of work, but as yet I have not had much experience. I have no high-hat ideas about salary. All I want is a toehold. I'll do the climbing after that.

Sincerely yours,

Bill Slangslinger

The writer's attempt to be lively only results in looking strange. And employers are looking for people with a sense of what is proper in certain situations. Therefore, we should learn to recognize slang and replace it with standard formal English when we are writing formal letters or reports.

Controlled Composition 17.1
Practice Changing Slang to Standard English

Rewrite the following passage, using standard English instead of slang. There is more than one way to do this, so you should consider the instructor's answer key just a suggested version. Your instructor can help you decide whether you are still using some slang, or you can check to see if the dictionary labels your words as slang.

Ups and Downs with a Chick
(Adapted from a story by Chuck Stroud, college student)

One morning as I was tooling my wheels down the white line from my pad to the sweat shop, I spotted a groovy chick whose heap had copped out. She caught my eye and flagged me down with a Kleenex. I hit the binders and swung over next to her gas hog. Since I'm noted for bombing out with chicks, I figured Big Daddy must be smiling down on me.

She wiggled over to me and said, "Man, am I glad to set eyes on you! I've always been turned on by the big, ugly dudes who can fix a bucket of bolts."

I spotted the square wheel on the right rear. "Cool it, Baby," I said. "If you've got a spare, we'll be flying right in no time."

She really turned on with that and gushed, "Simply fab! You're a real fox!"

Man, did I get with it! I changed that wide oval so fast it would put a tread-snatcher to shame. But as soon as I snapped the hubcap back in place, she socked it to me: "Thanks, Pal, but I've gotta split. My Old Man's waiting."

From "Ups and Downs with a Chick," an unpublished paper by Chuck Stroud. Reprinted by permission of Chuck Stroud.

Controlled Composition 17.2

Rewrite the following passage, using standard English instead of slang. There is more than one way to do this, so you should consider the instructor's answer key just a suggested version. Your instructor can help you decide whether you are still using some slang, or you can check to see if the dictionary labels some of your words as slang.

What's Wrong with Today's Rats?

Scientists must be on the wrong track, using rats for laboratory experiments. Today's rats are the crummiest choice they could make. To see what I mean, just stuff a rat with the equivalent of 400 cans a day of diet soda pop. It keels over. Or ask it to puff three packs of nonfilter-tip smokes a day. It goes belly-up. Pile cyclamates or saccharin on its Wheaties, and its tail might go plunk or its hair dribble away. It can't even handle ten or twelve martinis every night for 500 nights running without getting boozed up.

And just because these party-pooping drags can't handle modern living, the feds are trying to take away life's little pleasures from the human types. If today's rats can't stomach whipped cream, let's get rid of the rats, not the whipped cream. Maybe scientists ought to use Arabian stallions (now there's a hardy breed!) or, better still, houseflies.

Creating

17.3   Rewrite a paper you wrote in slang for Lesson 16, putting it completely into standard English.

17.4   Write two paragraphs about a funny experience you have had, putting one into slang and the other into standard English. Both paragraphs should tell the same story, but in different language.

DO NOT WRITE IN THIS BOOK

18

Using Not, Never, Neither, and Nor

What difference does one word make in these two statements?

I am going to run for office.
I am not going to run for office.

One word has changed the statement to the complete opposite. So *not* is a very important word, along with its other forms *do not (don't), will not (won't),* and *does not (doesn't).* When we want to be even more emphatic, we use *never,* meaning *not ever.*

Neither and *nor* are usually used together, and using them takes more skill than using *not. Either* and *or* are used together when we have one choice but not both; *neither* and *nor* are used together when we do not have either choice. Here are two simple examples:

1. You may have *either* soup *or* salad.
2. *Neither* soup *nor* salad is included with the meal.

Whatever follows *either* should be similar in structure (parallel) to whatever follows *or.* Similarly, what follows *neither* should be parallel to what follows *nor.* (If you need a review of parallel structure, look back at Lesson 15). The examples below use *neither* and *nor* with subjects, verbs, and prepositional phrases.

Subjects: *Neither* Lynn *nor* Larry was hurt.
Verbs: My dad *neither* likes *nor* understands jazz.
Prepositional phrases: We will give up *neither* to our enemies *nor* to our friends.

Clauses often use *not* and *nor* together instead of *neither* and *nor*. When they do, the clause following *nor* may turn its subject and verb around as in these examples:

1. We will *not* give in, *nor will we* give up.
2. He does *not* like jazz, *nor does he* understand it.

If we are not careful in using *neither* and *nor,* we may write some awkward and confusing sentences. The examples below are lined up to show clearly whether they are parallel (similar in structure) or not parallel. The first one awkwardly follows *neither* with a verb and *nor* with a prepositional phrase:

Poor: He *neither* asked me about my experience
     nor   about my references.

That sentence can be made better in two possible ways:

Better (with parallel phrases): He asked me *neither* about my experience
     nor   about my references.
Better (with parallel verbs): He *neither* asked me about my experience
     nor   checked my references.

Another skill you will need for using *neither* and *nor* has to do with choosing a verb when two subjects are joined by those words. You will remember that when two subjects are joined by *and,* we always use a plural verb because we are talking about more than one person or thing, like this:

John and Bill *were* both from Tehachapi.
Cleanliness and neatness *are* valued by employers everywhere.

But when subjects are joined by *neither/nor* or *either/or,* we are not always talking about more than one person or thing. We solve the problem by choosing the verb that goes with the closer subject, like this:

Neither the coach nor the players *were* satisfied. (players *were*)
Neither the players nor the coach *was* satisfied. (coach *was*)

Be careful about using *double negatives.* When two negative words are used together, they partly cancel each other out. For example, *unkind* means *not kind.* So if we say, "He frowned, but his voice was *not unkind,*" we mean that he wasn't exactly kind, but he wasn't exactly unkind either. That kind of double negative is quite clear and useful. But confusion can result in cases like the following:

1. **Confusing:** My kids *never* gave me *no* trouble.
   Better: My kids *never* gave me *any* trouble.
2. **Confusing:** He *hasn't* got *no* business here.
   Better: He *hasn't* got *any* business here.
3. **Confusing:** All their promises *don't* mean *nothing.*
   Better: All their promises *don't* mean *anything.*
   Or: All their promises mean *nothing.*
4. **Confusing:** Cora May *didn't* get *nothing* done today.
   Better: Cora May *didn't* get *anything* done today.
   Or: Cora May got *nothing* done today.

The words *hardly, barely,* and *scarcely* are negative words, too:

5. **Confusing:** Sam *couldn't hardly* lift the heavy sack.
   Better: Sam *could hardly* lift the heavy sack.
6. **Confusing:** She was so frightened she *couldn't scarcely* speak.
   Better: She was so frightened she *could scarcely* speak.

Be sure, however, to use a negative word when you really mean *not.* The following error is becoming very common:

7. **Confusing:** I *could care* less. (Then maybe you care a lot.)
   Better: I *couldn't care* less. (Then you must care very little.)

Be sure to say what you really mean.

Sentence Combining 18.0
Sentences with *Not/Nor* and *Neither/Nor*

A. **Combine the sentences below, using *not* and *nor.* Remember to turn the subject and verb around after *nor.***

Example: Doctor Taylor is not taking any new patients. He is not doing surgery any more.
Combined: Doctor Taylor is not taking any new patients, *nor is he* doing surgery any more.

1 Judge Scroggins would not let the jury go home. He would not let them see the newspapers.

_____

_____

2 The audience will not stop clapping. They will not be satisfied until the Groupies sing an encore.

_____

_____

3 The computer programmer does not know how the mistake happened. She cannot find anything wrong with the machine.

_____

_____

4 People are not willing to raise taxes. They are not willing to give up government services they are used to.

_____

_____

5 Those actors can't seem to remember their lines. They do not seem too concerned about it.

_____

_____

    B. Combine the sentences below, using *neither* and *nor*. Keep the structure parallel—that is, the same after *nor* as it is after *neither*. (When you use *neither* instead of *not*, don't turn the subject and verb around after *nor*.)

    Example: The manufacturer does not guarantee parts. He does not guarantee labor.

    Combined: The manufacturer guarantees *neither* parts *nor* labor.

    Note: The words *parts* and *labor* are parallel here. It would not be parallel to write, "The manufacturer neither guarantees parts nor labor," because *guarantee parts* (which follows *neither*) is not parallel to *labor* (which follows *nor*).

6 Steve was not in class today. Janet was not in class today.

_____

_____

7 Tony does not eat a balanced diet. He does not exercise regularly.

_____

_____

8 My girl friend did not answer my letters. She did not telephone me.

_____

_____

9 Senator Tubbs did not vote for tax reform. He did not vote for national health insurance.

_____

_____

10 Bill does not like camping. He does not enjoy traveling on a motorcycle.

_____

_____

Controlled Composition 18.1
Practice Using *Not, Never, Neither,* and *Nor*

Rewrite the following passage, changing it from a positive statement to a negative one. Use the words *not, don't, won't, never, neither,* and *nor*. In sentence 2, use *neither* and *nor*. In sentence 6, leave out *do not* and change *either* and *or* to *neither* and *nor*. In sentence 7, use *never*. Proofread to make sure all the statements would be likely to come from a person who does *not* like exercise and health foods.

Put a box around each of your changes, and have your instructor check them against the answer key. Your first two sentences, when changed, will look like this:

(1) I am ⬚not⬚ a health nut. (2) I ⬚neither⬚ jog every day ⬚nor⬚ play tennis twice a week.

The Health Nut

(1) I am a health nut. (2) I jog every day and play tennis twice a week. (3) I really like nutritious foods such as yogurt, bran cereals, whole grain breads, and raw fruits and vegetables. (4) I avoid cigarettes, alcohol, and foods that are made with white flour or loaded with sugar and salt. (5) I supplement my diet with vitamin and mineral tablets just in case my foods have been grown in soil depleted of the nutrients it once had. (6) I read labels on the products I buy to make sure they do not contain either food coloring or preservatives. (7) I always get eight hours of sleep at night, and when I'm under stress, I always meditate. (8) I hope to live to be a hundred years old. (9) I really call that living!

Controlled Composition 18.2

Rewrite the following passage, changing it from a positive statement to a negative one. Use the words *not, don't, won't, never, neither,* and *nor,* so that all statements would be likely to come from a person who does *not* believe that positive thinking does any good. In sentence 2, use *doesn't.* In sentence 4, use *neither* and *nor* instead of *both* and *and.* In sentence 5, use *never.* In sentence 9, use *neither* and *nor.* In sentence 10, use *don't* and *nor do I.* Proofread to make sure all the statements are negative. Put a box around each of your changes, and have your instructor check them against the answer key. Your first two sentences, when changed, will look like this:

(1) I am definitely ⬚not⬚ a positive thinker. (2) As I look all around me, I see evidence that the power of positive thinking ⬚doesn't⬚ really ⬚work.⬚

What I Think of Positive Thinking

(1) I am definitely a positive thinker. (2) As I look all around me, I see evidence that the power of positive thinking really works. (3) I have seen other people set high goals and achieve them just by telling themselves over and over that

they could do it. (4) This gives me both hope and confidence when setting goals of my own. (5) When I need help, I have always found other people willing to help me.

(6) I like the idea of moving toward my goals a little at a time, inch by inch. (7) Ten years from now, you probably will see me plugging along on a goal I started this year. (8) If the road turns out to be long and hard, I will just keep on going. (9) I have both the ability and the strength for it. (10) I expect to climb the ladder of success, and I hope to inspire my friends to climb it.

Creating

18.3   Think about a product you have used that did not come up to the claims of its advertisements. Then write an advertisement of your own telling what this product will not do, using words like *not, never, neither,* and *nor.* This can be a funny treatment of the subject.

18.4   Write a letter to a friend complaining about the weather where you live. Use words like *not, never, neither,* and *nor* or contractions like *can't, don't, didn't,* and *won't* to show what you can't do because of the weather.

LESSON
19

Using Words with Negative Connotations

Which of the following speakers does not like the governor and his plans?

Speaker One: The governor has many friends in the legislature who are using their influence to support his broad program for urban renewal.

Speaker Two: The guv has a bunch of cronies in the legislature who are using their political muscle to push through his big spending scheme to tidy up the slums.

Even though Speaker Two doesn't say it right out, we know he disapproves because of the negative words he uses (that is, words we associate with unpleasant ideas). For example, *guv* is not a respectful title; *cronies, political muscle, push through,* and *scheme* suggest some kind of unpleasant bullying. The words *big spending* and *slums* bring out the negative or unpleasant side of the problem rather than stressing the good the bill could do.

The first speaker uses pleasant or *positive connotations* (words we have good feelings about), and the second speaker uses *negative connotations* (words with unpleasant associations). When we write about something, we can make it sound good or bad depending on the words we choose. The following examples show how the same trait can be considered good or bad depending on whether we are describing ourselves, our friends, or someone we don't like:

Positive	Mildly Negative	Negative
I am firm.	You are stubborn.	He is pigheaded.
I am generous.	You are extravagant.	He is a spendthrift.
I am overweight.	You are chubby.	He is fat.

Similarly, a girl in love might lay her head *dreamily* on a pillow. But if the writer uses *wearily* instead of *dreamily*, he tells the reader she is tired and disappointed. In Controlled Composition 19.1, think especially about the connotations of *dreamily, magic night,* and *stars glittered joyfully.* In 19.2, think about the connotations of *trap* and *unsuspecting* in sentence 1.

Controlled Composition 19.1
Changing Positive to Negative Connotations

Rewrite the passage below, changing it from the best date to the worst date you ever had. Use words with negative or unpleasant connotations in place of words with pleasant connotations. Several versions are possible, of course, so the instructor's answer key should be considered only a suggested version. The important thing is to be consistently negative. Put a box around each of your changes, proofread to be sure the whole paper is consistent, and have it checked by your instructor. Here is one possibility for rewriting sentence 1:

His face was | unshaven, | and his smile was | yellow. |

The Best Date I Ever Had

His face was shaved, and his smile was radiant. He picked me up at 8:00 o'clock, right on time, and said a few courteous words to my mother. She obviously liked him.

Tom opened the door of his newly waxed car for me and helped me in. Seated in the back seat were the couple who were double-dating with us that magic night—Kevin and Christy, two delightful friends with a wonderful sense of humor.

I don't remember exactly what Tom said that night, but the conversation was warm and friendly, and he instantly made me feel comfortable. His jokes were witty, and he knew enough not to overdo them.

I remember that the dance music was fantastic, the hamburgers tasted marvelous, the stars glittered joyfully, the good-night kiss was tender, and before I laid my head dreamily on my pillow that night, I knew I was hopelessly in love.

Controlled Composition 19.2
Changing Negative to Positive Connotations

Pretend that you went to a restaurant that you liked but that your friend did not. Take the statement below, which your friend might have written, and change the negative words to positive or pleasing ones to make the restaurant sound appealing. Put a box around each of your changes. There are many words you could choose to do this assignment well, so your answer will not be exactly like the suggested version in the answer key. But proofread to be sure everything you have said gives a pleasant picture of the restaurant.

Your first sentence, when changed, might use *enjoyed* instead of *lived through,* and *restaurant* instead of *hash house.* How might you change the expression "trap the unsuspecting travelers"?

A Dinner at Selena's

Last night I lived through a dinner at Selena's, a hash house located near the freeway, where it can trap the unsuspecting travelers who make up most of its unfortunate customers. Does this eatery have atmosphere? It certainly does— loud music straight from the juke box, glaring lights overhead, a fireplace pouring out heat and smoke, the smell of sauerkraut drifting through the air. Does it have service? Yes, in the form of tight-skirted waitresses with ridiculous hairdos who never get your order right, who plunk your plate down when they serve you, and who refill your coffee cup if you holler at them to do it. Does it have good food? Yes, if you like leathery roast beef, cold mashed potatoes drowning in a tasteless gravy-mix, and lukewarm biscuits with whipped margarine. It's the kind of place you really can't believe until you've been there.

Creating

19.3   Using words with favorable or negative connotations, write about the best place or the worst place you ever lived in. Give enough details so that your readers can picture it in their minds.

19.4   Using words with favorable or negative connotations, write about the best party or the worst party you ever went to. Mention sounds and smells as well as sights to make your picture more complete.

19.5   Using words with favorable or negative connotations, write about the best job or the worst job you ever had. Give enough details so that your readers can imagine very clearly what it was like.

Writing About What People Say

When we write about what people say or have said, we are actually combining two sentences like these:

Two Sentences: Diane says something. She needs a ride.
Combined: Diane says that she needs a ride.

The combined sentence above is an example of *reported speech* because it is the form someone else uses to report what Diane says. Another way to combine the two sentences would be to show the exact words Diane uses. This is called *direct speech* because Diane says it directly to someone else. Direct speech uses quotation marks around her exact words, like this:

Diane says, "I need a ride."

If she has said this sometime in the past, we show that by using *said,* but we do not change the quoted words:

Diane *said,* "I need a ride."

However, if we were reporting her speech, we could put both verbs in the past, like this:

Diane *said* that she *needed* a ride.

Direct speech needs commas because it treats words like *she said* and *he replied* as sentence interrupters. Like other interrupters (which were explained in Lesson 13), these words are enclosed by two commas when they come in the middle of a quotation:

"If I don't find a ride," *she said,* "I can't go."

If words like *she said* come at the beginning or end of the quoted words, one comma is enough because we never begin or end a sentence with a comma. Here are two examples:

"If I don't find a ride, I can't go," she said**.**
"She said**,** "If I don't find a ride, I can't go."

Notice that the sentences in quotation marks begin with a capital letter, even if they do not start the main sentence.

If Diane's speech includes several sentences, we need quotation marks only before and after her whole speech, like this:

Diane said, **"**My car is broken down. I need a ride. If I don't find one, I can't go.**"**

However, if we interrupt the group of sentences with *she said,* we close the quotation with end quotation marks and open it again after the interrupter. Interrupters can also contain other modifying words, like this:

"My car has broken down,**"** *Diane said tearfully.* **"**I need a ride. If I don't find one, I can't go.**"**

Interrupters may come between the two halves of a compound sentence. In that case, we put the semicolon or the joining word after *said,* like this:

"My car has broken down, Diane said**,** "*and* I need a ride."
"My car has broken down," Diane said**;** "I need a ride."

Periods and commas always go inside quotation marks, possibly because they are very small and look neater that way. Other punctuation marks (such as question marks, exclamation marks, semicolons, and so on) go inside if they belong to the quotation and outside if they do not. In the first example below, the quoted words are a question, and the question mark goes inside the quotation marks. In the second example, the whole main sentence is a question, but the quoted words are not. So the question mark goes outside the quotation marks.

1. The manager asked, "Have you had experience**?**"
2. Did you ever hear him say, "I'm sorry"**?**

If the quotation ends with other punctuation, we don't need a comma before the interrupter, as in these two examples:

"Have you had experience**?**" the manager asked.
"I knew it**!**" Carol exclaimed.

Begin a new paragraph each time a different person begins to speak. That helps the reader to keep track of who is speaking. As long as the reader can easily tell who is speaking, we can sometimes leave out words like *he said.* Here is an example:

The manager put the application aside. "I'm sorry; we don't have any openings right now."

Sentence Combining 20.0
Combining Sentences for Direct Speech

A.   Notice how the following sentences can be combined.

Example: Jan said these words. "My family loves cats."
Combined: a. Jan said, "My family loves cats."
          b. "My family loves cats," Jan said.

Combine the sentences below in the same way, using commas, periods, capitals, and quotation marks correctly.

1 Jan said these words. "Cats are very clean animals."

a. _____

b. _____

2 Fernando asked this question. "Have you ever been to Los Angeles?"

a. _____

b. _____

3 Esther answered with these words. "No, but I'd like to see it."

a. _____

b. _____

B. Notice how this more difficult combination works, when an interrupter breaks into the middle of the quoted sentence.

Example: Millie said these words. "Jan must love cats, because she has three of them."

Combined: "Jan must love cats," *Millie said,* "because she has three of them."

Combine these sentences in the same way. (Notice that the interrupter is enclosed with commas and that two more quotation marks are needed.)

4 Joyce said these words. "Whenever we find a stray cat, we take it home."

_____

_____

5 Esther asked this question. "Have you ever lived in Los Angeles, and can you find your way around?"

_____

_____

6 Fernando answered with these words. "Yes, I lived there for five years."

_____

_____

C. Notice how this combination works when the speaker's words contain a semicolon.

Example: Lisa said these words. "My mother feels bad about giving away kittens; however, she makes sure they will have a good home."

Combined: "My mother feels bad about giving away kittens," Lisa said; "however, she makes sure they will have a good home."

Combine these sentences in the same way.

7 Tony said these words. "I'd like to have a cat; however, my landlord won't let me."

_____

_____

8 Coach Rodriguez said these words. "I know the score looks bad; nevertheless, we're playing to win."

_____

_____

9 Darlene said these words. "Dave hasn't eaten or slept for two days; how can he keep going like that?"

_____

_____

    D. **Notice how this combination works, when the speaker's words contain more than one sentence.**

      Example: Martha said these words. "I'm a good welder. Just give me a chance. I'll prove I can do a good job."
      Combined: "I'm a good welder," Martha said. "Just give me a chance. I'll prove I can do a good job."

Combine these sentences in the same way.

10 Manuel said these words. "Not all students can finish high school at eighteen. But they have a second chance. They can pass the G.E.D."

_____

_____

11 Mrs. Edgmon said these words. "Lots of students think they can't do math. But they have the ability. Only their fears are stopping them."

_____

_____

12 The shop manager asked these questions. "Have you had any experience? Where did you work last? Why did you leave?"

_____

_____

Controlled Composition 20.1
Practice Writing Direct Speech

DO NOT WRITE IN THIS BOOK

Rewrite the passage below, changing it from the form of a script to a story using direct speech. Use quotation marks, commas, and capital letters as needed. Remember to start a new paragraph when you change speakers. To be sure you get some practice with various ways of arranging sentences with quotations, follow these directions. In sentence 3, begin with the words *The manager asked,* (and so on). In sentence 4, end with *the woman replied.* In sentence 6, end with *he asked.* In sentence 7, begin with *Looking at the floor, she said,* (and so on). In sentence 8, begin with *The manager asked,* (and so on). In sentence 9, begin with *"Well," said the woman,* (and so on). In sentence 10, end with *the manager asked.* In sentence 11, begin with *Crossing her knees and* (and so on). In sentence 12, begin with *Putting the application on top of a large stack, the manager said,* (and so on). When you change sentences 3 and 4, they will look like this:

The manager asked,	**"** Have you filled out an application? **"**

" I don't have a pencil or pen with me **,"**	**the woman replied.**

An Interview with a Loser

(1) A young woman walked into the office of a clothing store, wearing a cotton T-shirt, faded jeans, and sandals without stockings. (2) When she was interviewed for a job, the following conversation took place.

(3) Manager: Have you filled out an application?

(4) Woman: I don't have a pencil or pen with me.

(5) The manager supplied a pen and waited while she filled out the form.

(6) Manager: Have you had any working experience?

(7) Woman: (looking at the floor) No.

(8) Manager: Is there any special reason you want to work in a clothing store?

(9) Woman: Well, I notice you don't open till ten in the morning.

(10) Manager: What kinds of work do you feel you could do best?

(11) Woman: (crossing her knees and leaning back in her chair) Oh, anything at all.

(12) Manager: (putting the application on top of a large stack) Well, thanks for coming in. (13) I really don't think I have anything to offer you right now.

Controlled Composition 20.2

Rewrite the passage below, changing it from a script to a story using direct speech. Use quotation marks, commas, and capital letters as needed. Remember to start a new paragraph whenever you change speakers. To be sure you get practice with various ways of arranging sentences with direct speech, follow these directions.

In sentence 3, begin with the words *The young man said,* (and so on). Begin sentence 5 with *Smiling, the manager said,* (and so on). In sentence 7, insert the interrupter *the young man replied* between *Naw* and *this.* End sentence 11 with *he said.* End sentence 13 with *Hank said.* End sentence 16 with *he asked.* In sentence 17, insert the interrupter *Hank answered* between *class* and *and.* Begin sentence 18 with *The manager asked,* (and so on). Begin sentence 19 with *Hank answered,* (and so on). End sentence 21 with *the manager said disgustedly.*

Put a box around each of your changes, proofread, and have your instructor check your paper against the answer key. When you have changed sentences 3 and 4, they will look like this:

The young man said, "The chick at the desk finally let me in to see you. I've been back three times now."

Interview with a Loser, No. 2

(1) Two young men, dressed in suits and ties, walked into the personnel office of Technical Industries, Inc. (2) When one of them was interviewed for a job, the following conversation took place.

Young man: (3) The chick at the desk finally let me in to see you. (4) I've been back three times now.

Manager: (smiling) (5) I guess you're serious about a job, then. (6) Are both of you applying?

Young man: (7) Naw, this here's my buddy Jim. (8) He just tagged along. (9) I'm Hank.

(10) The manager looked at Hank's application.

Manager: (11) You've had some welding courses, Hank. (12) How did you like them?

Hank: (13) They was okay. (14) I can learn most any kind of work.

(15) The manager saw the long list of jobs on Hank's application.

Manager: (16) What made you decide to become a welder?

Hank: (17) Jim here was in a welding class, and I tagged along.

Manager: (18) Are you familiar with the kinds of welding we do here?

Hank: (19) I don't know much about your company, but I can do any kind of welding. (20) How much do you pay?

Manager: (21) Union scale or better. (22) And now if you'll excuse me, I have some other people to interview.

Creating

20.3 Bosses, as well as employees, can have bad attitudes. You have done a controlled composition about an applicant for a job who shows a poor attitude. Now write about a boss with a bad attitude conversing with an employee who has made a mistake. Tell what each would say to the other, using quotation marks and proper punctuation for their words.

20.4 Write a conversation between a brother and sister. Have the older one try to convince the younger one to dress differently. Use quotation marks and proper punctuation for the words they speak to each other.

Changing Reported Speech to Direct Speech

Which of these sentences is more exciting?

1. Pecos Bill saw the rattlesnakes and asked me to hand him his gun.
2. Pecos Bill saw the rattlesnake. "Quick!" he cried. "Hand me my gun!"

Stories and novels are usually written with direct speech, also called *dialogue,* because it seems more real to the reader, as if he or she had actually been at the scene hearing the characters talk. Reported speech is useful at times, but it is usually not as interesting.

Reported speech can be changed into direct speech by deciding what the exact words of the speaker would be in that situation and putting them into quotation marks. Here is an example:

Reported: She thanked Gary and said that she would remember his kindness.
Direct: "Thank you, Gary," she said. "I'll remember your kindness."

Dialogue sounds more natural if we use interrupters like *he said* in places where speakers would naturally pause or take a breath.

Awkward and unnatural: "Well I notice," she said, "that you don't open till ten in the morning."

Natural sounding: "Well," she said, "I notice that you don't open till ten in the morning."

The best way to decide where to put *she said* is to speak the sentence aloud and listen for the natural breaks or pauses.

Controlled Composition 21.1
Using Quotation Marks for Direct Speech

Following the same rules that you learned in Lesson 20 about direct speech, rewrite the following passage of reported speech to use direct speech, properly punctuated with quotation marks, commas, and capital letters. You will need to figure out the exact words each speaker would say and put those exact words in quotation marks (they will be different from the words in the original passage below). Proofread to make sure you have used direct speech consistently, and have your instructor check your paper against the answer key. It should be very similar, although a few differences might be all right. When you have changed sentences 3 and 4, they should look very much like these:

3. "Have you filled out an application?" the manager wanted to know.
4. "Yes, I have," she replied, and gave it to him.

An Interview with a Winner

(1) A young woman walked into the office of a clothing store, wearing a neatly pressed blouse and smoothly fitting pants. (2) When she was interviewed for a job, the following conversation took place.

(3) The manager wanted to know if she had filled out an application. (4) She replied that she had, and she gave it to him. He said it looked good and complimented her on her neat handwriting. Smiling, she thanked him.

The manager asked if she had had any experience besides child care. She answered that she hadn't but that she had taken a lot of responsibility with children. She said that she had stayed with some children for as long as two weeks while the parents were away and added that she had listed some of her clients as references.

Seeming impressed, the manager continued his questioning. Did she have any special reason for wanting to work in a clothing store? She said that she did. She said that she loved clothes, and his store carried the kind of clothes she liked to wear herself.

He asked what kinds of work she felt she could do best. She said she could type a little but admitted she didn't like it very well. She would rather try selling, she said, because she liked working with people and helping them dress well. The manager said he liked her enthusiasm and asked how soon she could begin work.

Controlled Composition 21.2

Following the same rules that you learned in Lesson 20 about direct speech, rewrite the following passage of reported speech to use direct speech, properly punctuated with quotation marks, commas, and capital letters. Figure out the exact words each speaker would say, and put those exact words in quotation marks. (They will be different from the words in the original passage below.) Proofread to be sure you have used direct speech consistently, and have your instructor check your paper against the answer key. It should be very similar, though a few differences might be all right. When you have changed sentences 3, 4, and 5, they should look very much like these:

3–4. "Are you Mr. Garcia?" the young man asked. "I'm Charlie Sherman. Is this a good time to see you about a trainee job?"
5. "Yes," Mr. Garcia said. "May I have your application form?"

Interview with a Winner, No. 2

(1) A young man with neatly combed hair, wearing a clean sport shirt and slacks, entered the shop manager's office at Afford Motor Company. (2) When he was interviewed, the following conversation took place. (3) The young man asked the shop manager if he was Mr. Garcia and introduced himself as Charlie Sherman. (4) He asked if this was a good time to see him about a trainee job. Mr. Garcia said yes and asked Charlie for his application form. He looked at it and asked if Charlie had had any experience as a mechanic. Charlie said no, sir; that's why he wanted to work for Afford Motor Company. He'd heard they have a good training program.

Mr. Garcia asked why Charlie wanted to be a mechanic. Charlie replied that he'd always loved cars and anything mechanical, he'd taken auto shop in high school, and he'd earned a certificate of achievement in automotive mechanics at Bakersfield College. He admitted he wasn't too good at academic stuff.

Mr. Garcia asked if he read anything in his spare time. Charlie replied that he liked *Popular Mechanics, Newsweek,* and *Consumer Reports*. He also said he read the daily newspaper most of the time. Mr. Garcia said he liked Charlie's attitude. He told Charlie he'd check his references and call him on Wednesday.

Creating

21.3   Bosses, as well as employees, can have good attitudes. You have done a controlled composition about a winning attitude in an employee. Now write about a boss who shows an understanding attitude when his employee makes a mistake. Use quotation marks and proper punctuation for the words this boss and employee say to each other.

21.4   Write about the best advice anyone ever gave you, in the form of a conversation between you and that person. Use quotation marks and proper punctuation for the words you say to each other.

LESSON
22

Using Reported Speech

When we report to someone what another person has said, we often use reported speech instead of the exact words that were spoken. Then we can summarize the report and shorten it. Also, we don't need to make a separate paragraph every time we change speakers, as we do with direct or quoted speech. Paragraphing does make a passage easier to read, however, so make paragraphs out of groups of related sentences.

Direct speech can be turned into reported speech with several changes. The underlined words below are those that change in this process.

Direct: Jill said, "Some of my friends are looking for work. Should I send some down to apply?"

Reported: Jill said that some of her friends were looking for work. She asked if she should send some down to apply. (Whether can be used in place of if here.)

When we see the word *that* after *said*, we know it is reported speech, and it does not need quotation marks. However, we can sometimes leave out the word *that:*

Jill said that she agreed.   OR   Jill said she agreed.

No quotation marks are needed because the words *she agreed* are not the exact words she would speak.

In the above examples, both *said* and *agreed* are in the past tense. However, if the statement made is permanently true, we can use the present tense in that part of the sentence, like this:

Holly said (past tense) that a smile always helps (present tense).

She said everyone has some kind of skill.

Sentence Practice 22.0
Writing Sentences with Reported Speech

Change the following sentences from direct speech to reported speech.

Example: George asked, "Would you like a cheese omelette tonight, Al?"
"I'll eat it if you'll make it," Al replied.
Reported: George asked Al whether he would like a cheese omelette tonight. Al replied that he'd eat it if George would make it.

1 "Tomorrow night is your turn to cook," George reminded Al.

_____

_____

2 "I don't need to be reminded," Al said.

_____

_____

3 "What are you going to fix?" George wanted to know.

_____

_____

4 Al said, "I've got a can of spaghetti."

_____

_____

5 "I'm tired of spaghetti," George complained. "I'd like a shrimp salad and a spinach soufflé."

_____

_____

6 "I'd like that, too," Al agreed. "I suggest that we have some when it's your turn again."

_____

_____

Controlled Composition 22.1
Practice Using Reported Speech

Pretend you are reporting the conversation below to a friend, and write it that way in your notebook. Don't use any quotation marks, but follow the example of reported speech in Controlled Compositions 21.1 and 21.2 (Lesson 21). Proofread for consistency, and check your paper against the answer key. If it differs from the key, have your instructor check it. Some differences may be okay. Sentence 2, when changed, will look like this:

Jill said that some of her friends were looking for work and asked if she should send some down to apply.

How the Manager Hires an Employee

Holly Winn, Manager of Miller's Clothing, was talking to her friend Jill, a college student.

Jill: Some of my friends are looking for work; should I send some down to apply?

Holly: Sure, but tell them how to fill out an application.

Jill: What should I tell them?

Holly: First of all, they should fill it out completely. When they leave big blank spots, it looks as if they haven't thought about it or don't really care.

Jill: What do people usually leave out?

Holly: They quite often leave out experience and job skills, but almost everyone has some experience in volunteer work or church work or working for a neighbor. I think everyone can list some skills, like getting along well with others, talking well, or being good in math or English.

Jill: I agree. They just don't think to put those things down.

Holly: It also helps if they can spell and write legibly.

Jill: What else makes a good impression?

Holly: A smile goes a long way, and so do clean clothes, a bath, and a deodorant. Applicants should wear clothes appropriate for the job and talk in a pleasant way, not just grunt a word or two. They should seem eager to work, not lazy or full of complaints. And they should want especially to work for Miller's, enough to know something about the company. If you send me some like that, I'll be glad to hire them.

Controlled Composition 22.2

Pretend you are reporting the conversation below to some friends, and write it that way in your notebook. Don't use any quotation marks, but follow the example of reported speech in Controlled Compositions 21.1 and 21.2. Unlike direct speech, reported speech does not require changing paragraphs with every change of speaker. But you should group related sentences into logical paragraphs.

Proofread for consistency, and have your instructor check your paper against the answer key. Some differences may be okay. When changed, the second, third, and fourth sentences should look like this:

Larry asked Hiram what turns employers off in an interview . Hiram replied that the first thing they would notice is a dirty or careless appearance. They don't expect a mechanic to come in a suit and tie, but he should look neat and clean.

What Turns Employers Off?

Larry Finicky, an industrial arts teacher, was talking to his friend Hiram Wright, the personnel manager of a large industrial firm.

Larry: What turns employers off in an interview?

Hiram: The first thing we would notice is a dirty or careless appearance. We don't expect a mechanic to come in a suit and tie, but he should look neat and clean.

Larry: What else is important?

Hiram: The applicant's overall attitude is the most important thing. If he slouches and mumbles and doesn't seem ready to answer questions about what he can do or what tools he can use, we get the impression that he doesn't really want to work.

Larry: Is his English important?

Hiram: Good English always helps, especially for clerical jobs. It isn't as important for an electrician as it is for an office worker, but every worker should be able to explain himself clearly.

Larry: What kind of person makes the worst impression?

Hiram: We all dislike a rude, self-centered, dishonest, or phony person. If he can't get along with other workers, it doesn't matter how skillful he is. But if he's considerate and friendly, we can always help him improve his skills on the job.

Creating

22.3   Write a friend's opinion of a movie as you would report it to another friend. Use reported speech only, no quotation marks.

22.4   Find a newspaper or magazine article that uses quotations from a person being interviewed. Change a few paragraphs from direct speech to reported speech, using no quotation marks.

22.5   Take a comic strip and write a report of what the characters said to each other in the form of reported speech. For example: Lucy said that she would hold the football for Charlie Brown, but Charlie said he didn't trust her.

LESSON
23

Verb Variety, Using -ing Words

What is the difference in the meaning of these two sentences?

1. Dogs bark at cats.
2. The dogs are barking at the cats.

Sentence 1 is a fact permanently true (or at least generally true). But sentence 2 tells us certain dogs are doing something right now. When we write about what is going on right now, we use an *-ing* word in the verb, combined with one of these helper verbs: *am, is, are, can be, may be.* Examples:

I *am writing* a book.   He *is working* tonight.
You *are stepping* on my toe.   They *are playing* their guitars.
You *can be stamping* the envelopes while I *am folding* the letters.

Sometimes an adverb comes between the helper and the *-ing* word, as in these examples: (Remember that adverbs are modifiers, not helper verbs.)

You *are* not *bothering* me.   He *is* surely *kidding.*

When we write about what was going on at a certain moment in the past, we change the helper, but not the *-ing* word. Examples:

I *was trying* to reach you all last week.
Ella Fitzgerald *was performing* in New York last summer.
You *were sleeping* when Jerry called.
They *were* quietly *playing* their guitars as we sang.

To put a whole passage in the past, sometimes other words must be changed along with the verb, as in these examples:

1. I *am* waiting *here*. I *was* waiting *there*.
2. He *is* thinking he *can't* afford it. He *was* thinking he *couldn't* afford it.

The *-ing* word cannot be a verb unless it has a helper. The underlined phrases below are sentence fragments:

1. We were watching the baseball game. <u>The children playing happily</u>
   <u>nearby</u>.
2. I awoke suddenly. <u>The sun pouring in my windows</u>.

Fragments like these can be attached to the previous sentence as modifiers, like this:

I awoke suddenly, the sun pouring in my windows.

Or they can be made complete sentences with a helper verb, like this:

The children *were playing* happily nearby.
The sun *was pouring* in my windows.

Controlled Composition 23.1
Practice Using *-ing* Words in Verbs

The letter below tells a friend what is going on as the writer is writing. Pretend the vacation is now over, and those events are a memory. Rewrite the passage in the past. Put a box around your changes, proofread, and have your instructor check your paper against the answer key. Your first two lines, when changed, will look like this:

| I remember | my first night in Hawaii. My terrace | was | facing the ocean, and the sun | was | sending its last, long slanting rays across the sands below.

A Letter from Hawaii

Dear Brent:

This is my first night in Hawaii. My terrace is facing the ocean, and the sun is sending its last, long, slanting rays across the sands below. The waves are crashing on the pebbly beach, making restful music; the gulls and the crickets are adding their own notes to the chorus. They sound much nicer than the monotonous Hawaiian melodies that are blaring with a steady, dreary cheerfulness in the hotel lobby.

The winds are blowing gently from the west, bending the tops of six spindly palm trees. An older couple is strolling along the footpath, stopping now and then to pick up a seashell. Cotton-puff clouds are catching the last red rays of the sun.

Much to my surprise, Hawaii is living up to the promises in the travel folders. And I am sitting here wondering how any place on earth can be so perfect, and at the same time so perfectly terrible, and so terribly lonely, all because I am not sharing it with you.

Controlled Composition 23.2

Pretend you are a person who used to waste time but who has learned to use your time wisely. Pretend you are telling someone else what you used to do in the past. Rewrite the passage below, putting it in the past tense. Remember not to change the *-ing* word, only the verbs and helper verbs. Put a box around each of your changes, proofread, and have your instructor check your paper against the answer key. Your first sentence, when changed, will look like this:

I used to be a time-waster until I saw that I was letting the time-gobblers eat up a lot of my time.

Sentence 9, when changed, should read like this:

Clearly, the time-gobblers were controlling me when I should have been controlling them.

The Time-Gobblers

I can see that I am letting the time-gobblers eat up a lot of my time. The worst gobbler, television, is casting a spell on me and holding me long after my favorite programs are over. Unnecessary trips are also eating up my time; I am going to the store too often because I am not keeping a list of what I need and getting it all in one trip. My waiting time at doctors' offices or bus stops is not being used for reading books or writing letters. I am fussing too much over chores like laundry and cleaning. Disorganization is also gobbling my time. Because I am not putting away my clothes and tools promptly, I am wasting a lot of time hunting for them later. I am always putting things off, then wasting time worrying about why I am not getting them done. (9) Clearly, the time-gobblers are controlling me when I should be controlling them. I am not going to let that happen any more.

Creating

23.3   Pretend you are on a vacation. Write to a friend about what you are doing, using verbs with *-ing* words for what is happening right now.

23.4   Write a paragraph describing people's actions in a park, a restaurant, a lobby, a store, or other busy place. Use verbs with *-ing* words to show that the action is going on right now.

Verb Variety, Using Have and Has

Which of these sentences would suggest that the crash victims are still alive?

1. The victims survived for three days.
2. The victims have survived for three days.

In sentence 1, they may have died after three days. But sentence 2 suggests that they are continuing to survive. Here are other examples using *have* and *has* as helper verbs:

These carpets *have lasted* for ten years. (They are still lasting.)
It *has rained* for a week. (It is still raining.)
We *have been using* this shampoo for two years. (We are still using it.)
The movie *has been playing* for three weeks. (It is still playing.)

Even if the event is over, but related to something going on in the present time, we can use *have* and *has* with the verb, like this:

Dr. Maslow *has studied* many couples in order to write this book.
We *have driven* all night to get here on time.
Children who *have had* chickenpox can't get it again.
The citizens here *have* always *voted* conservatively.

Sentences using *have* and *has* may combine with a fact that is permanently or generally true. The combination works like this:

We *have known* something for years. Vitamin A *helps* eyesight.

The permanently true statement stays in the present tense, often in a clause beginning with *that,* and does not use *have* and *has.* It combines like this:

We *have known* for years *that* vitamin A *helps* eyesight.

Here are some other examples of this kind of combination:

It *has been found that* adults never *lose* the ability to learn.
Research *has shown* that working mothers *raise* children as well as non-working mothers *do.*
It *has* not yet *been proved* that hair dye *causes* cancer in humans.

On the other hand, some ways of mixing verb forms can be confusing. Notice the inconsistency in the examples below. The inconsistent sentence mixes the *have* form and the past tense. It sounds as if the couple told each other of their love in the past, but not now:

Inconsistent: They *have loved* each other deeply, and they *told* each other of their love.
Consistent: They *have loved* each other deeply, and they *have told* each other of their love.

-Ing phrases can also be changed with forms of *have,* like this:

Present Tense: *Being* sure of himself, he *does* not *worry* about competition.
Have Form: *Having been* sure of himself, he *has* not *worried* about competition.

24.0
Choosing the Right Verb Form

How do you choose the right verb form to go with the helpers *have* and *has?* The last part of the verb that uses these helpers is called the *past participle.* If the words *past participle* seem hard to remember, just put any verb you want to use into the slots of these sentence patterns, and you will realize what form you need:

I ——— today. I ——— yesterday. I have ——— many times before.
Example: I *eat* today. I *ate* yesterday. I have *eaten* many times before.

The last slot will then be filled by the past participle form. Usually, the past participle ends in *-ed,* just like the past tense. Some examples are *walked, needed, loved, shared,* and so on. Verbs like these that use *-ed* endings are called *regular verbs.* But some verbs have special forms for the past tense and the past participle. They are called *irregular verbs.* Here are a few examples:

Present Tense	Past Tense	Past Participle (to use with helpers *have* and *has*)
am, is	was	has been
are	were	have been
have	had	have had
drink	drank	have drunk
take	took	have taken
grow	grew	have grown
sleep	slept	have slept
speak	spoke	have spoken
tear	tore	have torn
go	went	have gone
swim	swam	have swum

A more complete list is given in the handbook section of this book, "Verb Tenses and Forms." A dictionary will also tell you when a verb has irregular forms. (Look up the present tense form, and it will give you any irregular forms as part of the definition.)

But remember, when you use *have* and *has* as helper verbs, use the right past participle, or the word that would go in the third column above. Your verb could also include an *-ing* word, as in "They *have been fighting* for two years," but don't worry about that for this lesson.

When we use *have* in a contraction, we shorten it to *'ve* like this:

I *should have* known = I *should've* known
We *could have* gone = we *could've* gone.
Donna *would have* been elected if she had run for office =
Donna *would've* been elected if she had run for office.

Because the *'ve* part of the contraction sounds like *of,* people sometimes get confused and write *would of* when they mean *would've,* or *could of* when they mean *could've.* But the word *of* is never a helper verb. In fact, it isn't a verb at all. Don't use *of* when you mean *have.*

Controlled Composition 24.1
Practice Using *Have* and *Has* as Helpers

Rewrite the passage below as if it were the twentieth anniversary of the couple described. Use the verb forms that have the words *have* and *has* before the main verb. Put a box around each of your changes, proofread for consistency, and have your instructor check your paper against the answer key. Your first two sentences, when changed, will look like these:

For the past twenty years, these two have had a self-actualizing marriage—the healthiest and happiest kind, according to Psychologist Abraham Maslow. They have loved each other deeply and have told each other often of their love.

The Best Kind of Marriage

These two have a self-actualizing marriage—the healthiest and happiest kind, according to Psychologist Abraham Maslow. They love each other deeply and tell each other often of their love. They share the same values, including honesty, kindness, and a sense of fairness. They realize that such values last although physical beauty may fade. Needing no pretenses, they are always natural and genuine. Needing no defenses, they are always open to their partner's point of view.

There is no competition between them; the husband takes pride in his wife's achievements just as she takes pride in his. They share household tasks and the care of their children. Being sure of their own sexuality, they do not worry about following rigid male or female roles.

Their sex life is playful and fun as well as a beautiful expression of love, but it is not the most important thing in their lives. Each accepts the other as an individual; each respects the other's differences. Although they enjoy each other immensely, each needs time to be alone. And their love grows deeper every year.

Controlled Composition 24.2

Pretend that the tennis team described in the passage below has been training for two months and is still training. Rewrite the passage, using the verb forms with *have* or *has* to show that this training has been going on for some time. Remember to keep the present tense for statements generally or permanently true, as in the last part of sentence 10:

He *has taught* them that an easy serve . . . *is* better than a fast serve . . .

Put a box around each of your changes, proofread, and have your instructor check your paper against the answer key. Your first two sentences, when changed, will look like this:

The tennis team ⌈ **has been** ⌉ getting in shape ⌈ **for two months,** ⌉ and soon they will be ready for league play. They ⌈ **have exercised** ⌉ every day, running three or four laps around the courts.

Training the Tennis Team

(1) The tennis team is getting in shape, and soon they will be ready for league play. (2) They exercise every day, running three or four laps around the courts. (3) They practice backhand and forehand shots in the handball courts. (4) They also practice with ball machines that throw to their backhand and their forehand. (5) They use up buckets of balls whenever they practice their serves. (6) They give up skiing because they could break some bones. (7) They stay away from cigarettes and alcohol because those poisons could shorten their breath. (8) The best players try to play as often as possible against other good players who give them a challenge and force them to do their best.

(9) Coach Lewis gives them good pointers and they listen. (10) For example, he teaches them that an easy serve to their opponent's backhand, followed by a rush to the net, is better than a fast serve to the forehand that can be returned fast. (11) He also shows them how to get a top spin on the ball to delay the return. (12) They are doing everything beautifully, and the coach is pleased with their progress.

DO NOT WRITE IN THIS BOOK

Creating

24.3   Write about something you have been doing or trying to do over a period of time, such as growing plants or improving an athletic skill or changing a habit. Use *have* and *has* with verbs to show that the action is continuing from the past into the present time.

24.4   Write about something your team, club, or organization has been doing over a period of time, such as building membership, doing service work, trying to change regulations, and so on. Use *have* and *has* in your verbs to show that the action has been going on and is continuing in the present time.

Verb Variety,
Using Had

In what order would these events usually occur?

1. Celebrated twentieth anniversary
2. Raised three children
3. Got married
4. Got engaged
5. Went steady
6. Had first date

For most couples, these events occur in the reverse of the order given above. All of these events took place in the past, but some took place earlier than others. We use *had* to place an event further back in time. Here are some examples:

1. By the time they got engaged, they *had gone* steady for a year.
2. By the time they celebrated their twentieth anniversary, they *had raised* three children.
3. Before they married, they *had known* each other for three years.
4. Until they met, they *had* never *been* truly in love.

The following sentences can show three different times when events occurred by using the proper forms of the verbs:

I *am* sorry (right now) that I *missed* you (yesterday).
When I *called* (yesterday), you *had* already *gone* to bed (before the time of the call).

Verbs using the *have* form can be put further back in time using *had*, like this:

1. Today is Tuesday, and it *has* been raining for a week.
   Today is Friday. By last Tuesday, it *had* been raining for a week.
2. These winds *have* been clocked at 70 miles per hour.
   By the time the storm ended, the winds *had* been clocked at 70 miles per hour.

Remember that a statement permanently true may be left in the present tense. Expressions like *had known* indicate an action completed in the past. Expressions like *have known* indicate action that continues into the present.

Controlled Composition 25.1
Practice Using *Had* with Verbs

Rewrite the passage below as if the writer had already finished college. Use the verb forms that have the word *had* before the main verb. Put a box around each of your changes, proofread to make sure you used *had* consistently throughout your paper, and have your instructor check it against the answer key. Your first two sentences, when changed, will look like these:

By the time I finished college, I had learned to concentrate better. I had learned to do one thing at a time and to cope with distractors both physical and emotional.

Improving Concentration

In order to finish college, I must learn to concentrate better. I must learn to do one thing at a time and to cope with distractors both physical and emotional.

Physical distractors have always surrounded me—pictures of my friends on my desk, letters needing to be answered, postcards from a pleasant vacation. All these have pulled my thoughts away from studying. They have to be put out of sight. I have always done homework drills with a radio or music playing, but college reading assignments and problem solving require more concentration. So I have to stop the music because energy is wasted in "tuning out" any kind of noise. And I have to give quiet study at least a two-week trial, because the discomfort of missing the noise can be a distractor until one gets used to it.

Nagging thoughts of undone chores have to be quieted, too. I must learn to clear my mind by getting short phone calls or brief tasks taken care of quickly and by making written lists of things to do later.

Although a mild amount of tension may actually improve concentration, powerful emotions like pain, fear, and worry have distracted me at times. Fortunately, the college has a counselor to help me through really bad times.

Controlled Composition 25.2

Rewrite the first paragraph below (sentences 1 through 8) as if all this had happened before Robert Schumann became a composer. Begin sentence 1 with *Long before he became a composer.* Use the verb forms that have the helper *had* before the main verb. Leave the second paragraph (sentences 9, 10, and 11) just as they are.

Put a box around each of your changes, proofread to be sure you have been consistent in time with your verbs, and have your instructor check your paper against the answer key. Your first two sentences, when changed, will look like this:

(1) Long before he became a composer, Robert Schumann had wanted to become a famous pianist. (2) He had shown great musical talent at an early age, and his family had provided the best music teachers.

The Disappointed Musician
(Adapted from *The Wonderful World Within You*, by Roger Williams)

(1) Robert Schumann wanted to become a famous pianist. (2) He showed great musical talent at an early age, and his family provided the best music teachers. (3) He also showed a great desire to succeed, and he practiced up to seven hours a day. (4) Yet he was not able to reach his highest goal—to become the best-known concert pianist of his day. (5) Unlike other pianists, he had unusual difficulty with some of the fingers of his right hand. (6) According to some reports, he even injured his hand in his efforts to make it behave. (7) Eventually he gave up his dream. (8) His disappointment caused him to turn to composing the beautiful music that later made him famous.

(9) Today we know about differences in hand muscles that had not been discovered in Schumann's lifetime. (10) If he had known then what we know now, he would not have been so disappointed. (11) But his life proves that a disappointment can be turned into a triumph.

From *The Wonderful World Within You* by Dr. Roger J. Williams. Copyright © 1977 by Dr. Roger J. Williams. Reprinted by permission of Bantam Books, Inc. All rights reserved.

Creating

25.3   Write about how you got interested in your present work, hobby, or major field of study. Use the *had* form of the verb in at least a few sentences, as in this example: "Before I heard about this job, I *had* been working as a salesclerk."

25.4   Write about a change in your attitude from one that you formerly had, using the *had* form in a sentence something like this: "By the time I . . . , I had lost interest in . . ." Examples: *By the time I left high school, I had lost interest in cheerleading. By the time I could afford to date her, I had lost interest in Dolores. By the time I finished the book, I had decided I wanted to become a pilot.*

Writing About Two Past Events

It is easy to change a sentence from present to past, like this:

Present: *Come* in, *sit* down, and *have* some coffee.
Past: She *came* in, *sat* down, and *had* some coffee.

When we are already writing a story in the past tense, we need the *had* form to put some events even further back in the past. So we may be using the past tense and *had* forms in the same sentence, like this:

1. Before Linda *arrived* at ten, her mother *had* already *come* in and *had had* some coffee.
2. By the time the doctor *saw* him, Fred *had waited* an hour.
3. Until the clock *struck* twelve, Cinderella *had had* a ball.

If a whole series of events requires *had*, we can use *had* with the first item in the series and not repeat it. In the examples below, the *had's* in parentheses may be left out and just understood:

Before Linda arrived, her mother *had* come in, (had) put away her luggage, and (had) made a pot of coffee.

You may recall from Lesson 20 that we could put reported speech into the past, but direct speech stays exactly the way it was spoken. Similarly, we can use *had* with reported speech, but not with direct speech, unless, of course, it was part of the words actually spoken:

Reported Speech: My boss *said* yesterday that he *had been* impressed with my work on the Williamson account.

Direct Speech: Yesterday my boss *said,* "I *have been* impressed with your work on the Williamson account."

Controlled Composition 26.1
Practice Writing About Two Past Events

The story below is written in the present, as if it is going on right now, but it refers to earlier events. Rewrite it in the past, putting the earlier events further back in time by using *had* with the verbs instead of *have* or *has*. Remember that *had* is used only for events that happened before the other events in the main story. Put a box around each of your changes, proofread for consistency, and have your instructor check your paper against the answer key. Your first sentence, when changed, will look like this:

After they ⬛ had ⬛ taken their morning stroll, the three hippie bears ⬛ entered ⬛ their pad. (The stroll took place before the bears entered.)

The Three Hippie Bears
(Adapted from a story written by Keith Parker, college student)

After they have taken their morning stroll, the three hippie bears enter their pad. They find three bowls of granola, which they have left to cool. One bowl has been completely gobbled up. So they know some creep has been there. They walk into the TV room and eyeball their three chairs. All of them have been messed with, and one of them has been totaled out. So they know some fanny has flopped in them.

They tiptoe into the X-rated room and look over the scene. Big Daddy Bear comments that some jerk has rumpled the cover on his hard pallet. Momma Bear complains that some turkey has put a dent in her soft pillows. Teeny Bopper Bear exclaims, "There's a bod in my bed. Like wow!"

Momma Bear stops Teeny Bopper before he climbs in, too. Just then, Goldi-locks wakes up and sizes up the situation. She breaks out and splits the scene like lightning. The bears are a little shook up, but they don't let this happening ruin their day.

From "The Three Hippie Bears," an unpublished story by Keith Parker. Reprinted by permission of Keith Parker.

Controlled Composition 26.2

When we write about the ideas in a book, we can use the present tense (The author *says* this) or the past tense (The author *said* this). When we use the past tense, we must use the *had* form for events that came earlier. The passage below is written in the present with *have* and *has* forms. Rewrite it, using the past tense and *had* forms.

Put a box around each of your changes, proofread for consistency, and have your instructor check your paper against the answer key. Your first sentence, when changed, will look like this:

In his book *Life After Life*, Raymond Moody told about people he had interviewed who had come so close to death that their hearts had stopped beating, yet who had lived to tell about it.

Is There Life After Life?
(Adapted from *Life After Life,* by Raymond Moody)

In his book *Life After Life,* Raymond Moody tells about people he has interviewed who have come so close to death that their hearts have stopped beating, yet who have lived to tell about it. Although no two persons' stories are exactly the same, all of them have a number of things in common. A typical experience goes like this:

The dying person feels that he is out of his body. He looks down on it and sees the people who are trying to save him. He also feels that he is moving very fast through a kind of tunnel. At the end of this journey he finds a feeling of great peace and love. He sees a Being of Light that can communicate without words. The Being asks what the dying person has learned in his lifetime and how much he has loved. The person sees his whole life, the selfish and the unselfish parts, but the Being accepts it all. He gives the dying person a choice—to stay or to return to Earth. The person returns because he feels he has left unfinished business here, but he has been changed deeply. He has completely lost his fear of death, but he also wants more meaning in his life. He wants to learn all he can and to love all he can.

From *Life After Life* by Raymond A. Moody, Jr. Reprinted by permission of Mockingbird Press, Covington, Georgia 30209.

Creating

26.3   Retell a familiar story or fairy tale as you did in the controlled composition of "The Three Hippie Bears," using both the past tense and *had* forms of the verb. Use slang expressions if you wish.

26.4   Write about a sports event in the past and things that led up to it, using the *had* form of the verb. Example: The Renegades *won* the game, but only after they *had* put in several weeks of practice on new strategies.

26.5   Write about a person you know who has overcome a handicap, using both the past tense and *had* forms of the verb. Example: He *fought* back to life after the doctors *had* almost given up on him.

LESSON
27

Verb Variety, Using the Active Voice

In most English sentences, the subject does something to someone or something else, as in these examples:

The mice ate all our cheese.
Parents love their children.
The Red Sox won the game easily.

Because the subjects are performing the actions (of eating, or loving, or winning), we say these sentences are in the *active voice*. But sometimes we change the normal word order so that the subject is acted upon by someone or something else, as in the examples below (notice how the verb changes when we do this):

All our cheese was eaten by mice.

Children are loved by their parents.

The game was won easily by the Red Sox.

In this form, the subjects (cheese, children, game) are passively being acted upon (by the mice, the parents, or the Red Sox), so we say that these sentences are in the *passive voice*. The doers of the action are mentioned in the phrase starting with *by*. These by-phrases can be left out, however, so we may not know who or what has done the acting upon the subject, like this:

The game <u>was</u> easily <u>won</u>.

Children <u>are loved.</u>

All our cheese <u>was eaten</u>.

The active voice is usually stronger because it is less wordy, and it tells who is performing the actions. We change the passive voice into the active voice by deciding who or what would do this and making that person or thing the subject. This is very easy if the passive sentence contains a by-phrase. Here are some examples:

Passive: The company records <u>are kept</u> by the accountant.

Active: The accountant <u>keeps</u> the company records.

Passive: My motorcycle <u>was repaired</u> by expert mechanics.

Active: Expert mechanics <u>repaired</u> my motorcycle.

If we do not have a by-phrase, we can add any subject that makes sense, like this:

1. **Passive:** Today students <u>are</u> not <u>given</u> enough written work.

    Active: Today <u>our schools</u> do not <u>give</u> students enough written work.

2. **Passive:** Every child <u>must be loved</u> before he can learn to love.

    Active: <u>Someone</u> <u>must love</u> a child before he can learn to love.

In changing from passive to active voice, be sure to keep the same tense (that is, present or past), like this:

1. This book <u>is rated</u> excellent by the critics. (passive voice, present tense)

    The critics <u>rate</u> this book excellent. (active voice, present tense)

2. Last year this book <u>was rated</u> excellent by the critics. (passive voice, past tense)

    Last year the critics <u>rated</u> this book excellent. (active voice, past tense)

If you tend to be confused by words like *voice* and *tense,* don't worry about them. Just ask yourself, "Am I being consistent in writing about the past or about the present?" Then your inner common sense about language will guide you to make the right choice.

Sentence Practice 27.0
Changing from Passive to Active Voice

A. Notice how easily the passive voice can be changed to active when it has a by-phrase.

Passive: At 6:00 the news is reported by Walter Concrete.

Active: At 6:00 Walter Concrete reports the news.

Change the following sentences to the active voice. Keep them in the present tense as they are now; do not put them in the past.

1 (passive) Baby Stickleback fish are raised by their fathers.

(active) _____

_____

2 (passive) The hall is decorated by the dance committee every Friday.

(active) _____

_____

3 (passive) I am shocked by some of the new movies.

(active) _____

_____

4 (passive) A student like Arthur is not satisfied by a passing grade.

(active) _____

_____

5 (passive) Every television set is inspected by a technician before it leaves the factory.

(active) _____

_____

B. Change the following sentences to the active voice, keeping them in the past tense. (*Caution:* **Don't use** *have,* **has,** and *had* **in these sentences.**)

Passive: Fifty houses were damaged by the storm.

Active: The storm damaged fifty houses.

6 (passive) The White Sox were defeated by the Red Sox.

(active) _____

_____

7 (passive) The missing child was found by the police.

(active) _____

_____

8 (passive) A slow ball was thrown by the pitcher.

(active) _____

_____

9 (passive) We were almost killed by that crazy driver.

(active) _____

_____

10 (passive) The people were warned by the Surgeon General that cigarettes could cause cancer.

(active) _____

_____

C. When we do not have a by-phrase, we must supply a subject to turn the passive voice into the active voice.

Passive: Sometimes our freedoms are not fully appreciated.

Active: (subject we) Sometimes we do not fully appreciate our freedoms.

Change the following sentences to the active voice by adding the subject suggested below. *Caution:* **Do not use** *have, has,* **or** *had* **in these sentences.**

11 (passive) The fight was stopped in the sixth round.

(active, subject the referee) ⎯⎯⎯⎯⎯⎯⎯⎯⎯⎯⎯⎯⎯⎯⎯⎯⎯⎯⎯⎯

⎯⎯⎯⎯⎯⎯⎯⎯⎯⎯⎯⎯⎯⎯⎯⎯⎯⎯⎯⎯⎯⎯⎯⎯⎯⎯⎯⎯⎯⎯⎯⎯⎯⎯⎯⎯⎯

12 (passive) The Yankees are expected to win the pennant this year.

(active, subject fans) ⎯⎯⎯⎯⎯⎯⎯⎯⎯⎯⎯⎯⎯⎯⎯⎯⎯⎯⎯⎯⎯⎯⎯⎯

⎯⎯⎯⎯⎯⎯⎯⎯⎯⎯⎯⎯⎯⎯⎯⎯⎯⎯⎯⎯⎯⎯⎯⎯⎯⎯⎯⎯⎯⎯⎯⎯⎯⎯⎯⎯⎯

13 (passive) Ten motorists' lives were taken over the Labor Day weekend.

(active, subject accidents) ⎯⎯⎯⎯⎯⎯⎯⎯⎯⎯⎯⎯⎯⎯⎯⎯⎯⎯⎯⎯⎯⎯

⎯⎯⎯⎯⎯⎯⎯⎯⎯⎯⎯⎯⎯⎯⎯⎯⎯⎯⎯⎯⎯⎯⎯⎯⎯⎯⎯⎯⎯⎯⎯⎯⎯⎯⎯⎯⎯

14 (passive) After all the ballots are counted, the celebrations begin.

(active, subject the workers) ⎯⎯⎯⎯⎯⎯⎯⎯⎯⎯⎯⎯⎯⎯⎯⎯⎯⎯⎯⎯⎯

⎯⎯⎯⎯⎯⎯⎯⎯⎯⎯⎯⎯⎯⎯⎯⎯⎯⎯⎯⎯⎯⎯⎯⎯⎯⎯⎯⎯⎯⎯⎯⎯⎯⎯⎯⎯⎯

15 (passive) The typing was not completed until Saturday morning.

(active, subject my secretary) ⎯⎯⎯⎯⎯⎯⎯⎯⎯⎯⎯⎯⎯⎯⎯⎯⎯⎯⎯⎯

⎯⎯⎯⎯⎯⎯⎯⎯⎯⎯⎯⎯⎯⎯⎯⎯⎯⎯⎯⎯⎯⎯⎯⎯⎯⎯⎯⎯⎯⎯⎯⎯⎯⎯⎯⎯⎯

D. Change the following sentences from the passive to the active voice. These all have more than one helper verb.

Passive: Over 50,000 cars have been sold already this year.

Active: Dealers have sold over 50,000 cars already this year.

16 (passive) So far, Professor Dabbs has been impressed by his students.

(active) _____

_____

17 (passive) Forty-five Hispanics have been appointed to office by the President.

(active) _____

_____

18 (passive) During World War II, many "men's jobs" were being done by women.

(active) _____

_____

19 (passive) When everything had been done to make Roger comfortable, she sat
    quietly by his bedside.

(active) (subject she) _____

_____

20 (passive) No higher honor could have been paid to a soldier by a grateful
    country.

(active) _____

_____

Controlled Composition 27.1
Practice Changing from Passive to Active Voice

Rewrite the passage below, changing from the passive voice to the active
voice wherever possible. You will need to change all the verbs that are
underlined to give them a different subject than they now have. Put a box
around each of your changes, proofread to be sure the whole paper makes

sense, and have your instructor check it against the answer key. Sentences 1 and 2, when changed, will look like this:

Combat soldiers who had to spend long, boring hours in foxholes $\boxed{\text{invented}}$ the game called "Hinky Pinky." Anyone $\boxed{\text{could play}}$ it.

The Foxhole Game

The game called "Hinky Pinky" <u>was invented</u> by combat soldiers who had to spend long, boring hours in foxholes. It <u>could be played</u> by anyone. No special equipment <u>was needed</u> by the players.

This is how the game <u>was played</u> by the men. One person just thought of two words that rhyme, such as "blue shoe." Then a definition <u>was given</u> to the other players, such as "colored footwear," and they had to think of the two rhyming words that fit the definition.

Players <u>were given</u> even greater challenges by two-syllable rhyming words. For example, the definition "glass weapon" stood for "crystal pistol," and "a poorly dressed taxi driver" stood for "a shabby cabby." Even some three-syllable hinky-pinkies <u>were made up</u> by the soldiers. What, for instance, is a "live-in officer"? You guessed it—a "resident president," of course.

Controlled Composition 27.2

Rewrite the passage below, changing from the passive to the active voice wherever possible. You will need to change all the verbs that are underlined and give them a different subject than they now have. Put a box around each of your changes, proofread to make sure the whole paper makes sense, and have your instructor check it against the answer key. Sentences 1 and 4, when changed, will look like this:

1. The narcissist (pronounced NAR-sis-ist) $\boxed{\text{derives}}$ $\boxed{\text{his name}}$ from a Greek legend about Narcissus, a handsome boy who fell in love with his own reflection in a pool.

4. Once $\boxed{\text{he establishes}}$ his own self-esteem, he no longer needs so much attention from others.

The Narcissist

(Adapted from an article in *Psychology Today* by Linda Wolfe)

(1) The name of the narcissist (pronounced NAR-sis-ist) <u>is derived</u> from a Greek legend about Narcissus, a handsome boy who fell in love with his own reflection in a pool. (2) Every child <u>must be loved</u> by other persons before he can learn to love in return. (3) His ego <u>is fed</u> by admiration and approval. (4) Once his own self-esteem <u>is established</u>, he no longer needs so much attention from others.

But the narcissist <u>is</u> not <u>satisfied</u> by the love of family and a few friends. Other people <u>are</u> constantly <u>used</u> by him for the attention they give him; then they <u>are tossed</u> aside. Although he seems to love himself too much, he really doesn't love himself enough, and so he thinks constant reassurance <u>is needed</u>. His possessions, talents, or intelligence <u>are displayed</u> in ever-increasing amounts to get more and more attention.

The narcissist <u>can be treated</u> by a psychologist, but usually not until he is in his forties or fifties. Then he can see that his life is empty and meaningless, and he may be willing to change.

Reprinted from *Psychology Today* Magazine, copyright © 1978 Ziff Davis Publishing Co. Reprinted by permission.

Creating

27.3 Describe a scene of high activity, using the active voice for all verbs to help create a sense of that great activity. Some examples might be an exciting event on a highway, part of a sports event, bustling Christmas shoppers, a playground fight, fighting a fire, running a race, competing in a contest, or any other exciting experience.

LESSON
28

Verb Variety, Using the Passive Voice

Although the active voice is usually better and stronger, there are times when we need the passive voice to emphasize the receiver of an action. Here are some examples in which the passive voice is better:

1. This restaurant *is known* for its French onion soup.
   (We don't care who knows it; it's the restaurant that's important.)
2. Shakespeare *was buried* at Stratford.
   (Shakespeare is more important than the gravediggers who buried him.)
3. Many small businessmen *are forced* to close their doors every year.
   (It may be vague economic forces like supply and demand that are forcing them, but we can't be sure, so we can't very well make up a subject to put this sentence into the active voice. It's better in the passive voice, emphasizing the businessmen.)
4. Over 150,000 mopeds *were sold* last year.
   (The number of mopeds sold is more important than the salespersons or companies that sold them.)

The controlled compositions in this lesson are just the opposite of those in Lesson 27. You will change several sentences from the active voice to the passive voice. Remember that you may do this in two ways, with or without a by-phrase, but include the by-phrase if it gives important information. Here are some examples:

1. Over 150,000 mopeds were bought *by Americans* last year. (This by-phrase gives important information.)
2. Some other limitations are also mentioned *by these owners*. (Obviously, the owners have been mentioned in a previous sentence, so we can leave out this by-phrase.)

It may help you to look closely at more examples of verbs in the passive voice, like these:

am invited	was kept	are supposed to	is being made
is loved	were sold	is used	was being done
are shared	was taught	has been known	will be bought
was invented	were given	have been told	can be ordered

Notice that the helper must include a form of the verb *be* (*am, are, is, was, were, will be, can be, has been, have been, is being,* and so on). The helper *have* alone does not make a verb passive; it must be combined with *been.* The sentence *We have eaten* is not passive, but *The oranges have been eaten* is passive because it includes *been,* a form of *be.* (Also look at the meaning; the subject is doing the acting in *We have eaten,* and the subject is being acted upon in *The oranges have been eaten.*) Although the word *got* is sometimes used in a passive verb in place of *be* (for example, *John got hit* instead of *John was hit*), this is very informal and should not be used in formal writing.

The verb in the passive voice must also end in a past participle, not in an *-ing* word. *We are eating* is not passive, but *The food is being eaten* is passive, because it ends in a past participle. You may remember from Lesson 24 that the past participle is the part of a verb that would fill this slot:

He has ——— many times before.

You do not need to analyze the verbs, however, if you just remember the main purpose of the passive voice—to show the subject receiving action by someone or something else, not doing the acting.

Sentence Practice 28.0
Changing from Active to Passive Voice

A. **Change to following sentences from the active to the passive voice. Keep them in present tense as they are now. Use by-phrases.**

Active: Some volunteers *give* blood regularly.
Passive: Blood *is given* regularly by some volunteers.

1 Campers destroy countless wildflowers every year.

_____

_____

2 The neighbors consider Marty a little crazy.

_____

_____

3 Many nationally known artists use Brandish Brushes.

_____

_____

4 The Anderson family sponsors several foreign students.

_____

_____

5 Selfish people rarely find happiness.

_____

_____

B. Change the following sentences from the active to the passive voice. Keep them in the past tense as they are now. Use by-phrases.

Active: Americans _bought_ over 150,000 mopeds last year.
Passive: Over 150,000 mopeds _were bought_ by Americans last year.

6 A teacher's aide graded the tests.

_____

_____

7 The basketball team scored over 100 points tonight.

_____

_____

8 The photographer took twenty wedding pictures.

_____

_____

9 Lorraine played the wedding march.

_____

_____

10 The guests threw handfuls of rice.

_____

_____

C. **Change the following sentences into the passive voice without a by-phrase. Keep the tenses the same as in the original sentences.**

Active: We find black bears in North American forests.
Passive, Without By-Phrase: Black bears *are found* in North American forests.

11 Someone notified the public that the schools would open September 7.

_____

_____

12 Someone draped a flag over the coffin.

_____

_____

13 Someone believes the vase to be over 1,000 years old.

_____

_____

14 In a proper table setting, one places the fork on the left.

_____

_____

15 In India, people consider all life to be sacred.

_____

_____

D. The following sentences contain one or more helper verbs. Change them into the passive voice, keeping the tenses the same as in the original sentences. Leave out the by-phrases.

Active: One *should plant* corn in rows.
Passive: Corn *should be planted* in rows.
Active: Someone *should have told* me.
Passive: I *should have been told*.

16 One *can double* this recipe to feed ten people.

_____

_____

17 Other suppliers *cannot surpass* the quality of Ultrasound Radios.

_____

_____

18 When they *have heard* all the arguments, the jury will go into the jury room to make a decision.

_____

_____

19 The company *has increased* your credit limit.

_____

_____

20 By the year 2000, someone *will have invented* a new kind of car.

_____

_____

Controlled Composition 28.1
Practice Using Passive Voice

Rewrite the passage below, changing the following sentences from the active to the passive voice: sentences **2, 3, 4, 5, 8,** and the first half of sentence **10.** Put a box around each of your changes, proofread to be sure the whole paper makes sense, and have your instructor check it against the answer key. If your paper is different from the key, talk to your instructor about it. Sentence **3,** when changed, will look like this:

Over 150,000 mopeds | were bought by Americans | last year, and more than double that number | are expected to be sold | this year.

Why Mopeds Are Popular
(Adapted from an article in *Consumer Reports*)

(1) The moped, a little motor-driven bicycle that can run all over town on a cup of gasoline, thrives where fuel is scarce and expensive. (2) That's why Europeans buy mopeds in great numbers. (3) Americans bought over 150,000 mopeds last year, and manufacturers expect to sell more than double that num-

ber this year. (4) Until recently, we imported all mopeds, but now some American companies are manufacturing them.

(5) Owners consider the moped just right for little errands that normally require the use of a car. (6) The main drawback mentioned is that mopeds, like bicycles, are practical only in good weather. (7) Even so, many people are happy to use a moped in place of a second car.

(8) Owners also mention some other limitations. (9) Its low speed makes the moped unsuitable (and probably unsafe) on freeways, in tunnels, and for long trips. (10) These limitations might discourage some potential buyers, but others will find the quiet, simple, and economical little moped a great convenience as gasoline becomes increasingly scarce and costly.

Copyright © 1978 by Consumers Union of United States, Inc., Mount Vernon, NY 10550. Excerpted by permission from *Consumer Reports,* June 1978.

Controlled Composition 28.2

Sometimes it is desirable to remove the word *I* from your writing to avoid seeming self-centered or to seem more factual. The passive voice can be used for this purpose, usually without by-phrases. Rewrite the passage below without using the pronouns *I* or *me* and without by-phrases. Ordinarily, we do not see the passive voice in every sentence of a passage (see exercise 28.1, for example). But in this special exercise you can make every sentence passive. In fact, sentences 2, 4, 6, and 11 all have more than one verb that you can make passive.

Put a box around each of your changes; proofread to see that you have not used *I* or *me* and that the paper makes sense. Then have your instructor check it against the answer key. Sentences 1 and 2, when changed, will look like this:

(1) Enough vegetables $\boxed{\text{can be grown}}$ in a small yard to feed a family of four. (2) First, good topsoil $\boxed{\text{is obtained}}$ and a box $\boxed{\text{built}}$ around it for good drainage.

A Vegetable Garden in a Small Space

(1) I can grow enough vegetables in a small yard to feed a family of four. (2) First I obtain good topsoil and build a box around it for good drainage. (3) I plant carrots and beets early in the spring. (4) I spread the seeds in an area about three feet square and cover them with topsoil and nitro humus. (5) I leave another square beside it to be planted two weeks later, so that a new crop is

always coming up. (6) When I have eaten the carrots from the first square, I plant a second crop of beets in that space. (7) I can rotate lettuce the same way, so that two dozen heads are ready to eat and new ones are coming up. (8) I need only a few bell peppers and tomato plants. (9) I place hog-wire hoops around the tomato plants to brace them as they grow. (10) I can discourage cutworms and other pests with a line of pesticide sprinkled around the garden's edge. (11) If I water it every morning, weed it a little each day, and fertilize it at least once, the garden will provide fresh vegetables until frost comes.

Creating

28.3   Using the passive voice wherever possible and underlining the verbs when you do, write a paragraph about a product that *was invented* to fill some human need. Tell how it *was developed,* what problems *were overcome,* how it *was sold* to the public, and so on. Examples might be the electric light, the telephone, the radio, polyester fabrics, or any other product you know about. You may look up information in an encyclopedia or other references.

28.4   Using the passive voice wherever possible and underlining the verbs when you do, write a paragraph or two about a product you would like to invent. Tell how it *will be developed,* what kinds of people *will be* served by it, how many you expect *will be sold,* and so on. You can make this assignment funny if you wish.

28.5   Write a report of a laboratory experiment, avoiding the use of *I.*

Writing a Business Letter

Your letters should contain these essential parts:

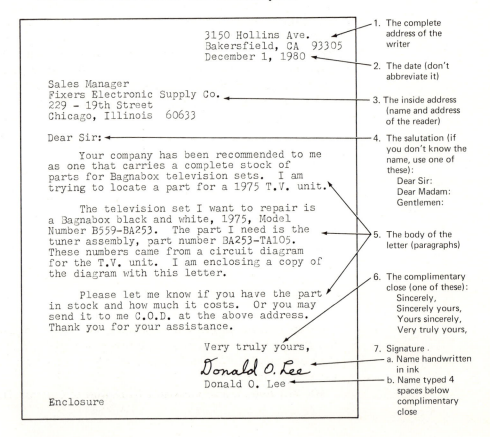

```
                                  3150 Hollins Ave.
                                  Bakersfield, CA  93305
                                  December 1, 1980

Sales Manager
Fixers Electronic Supply Co.
229 - 19th Street
Chicago, Illinois  60633

Dear Sir:

        Your company has been recommended to me
as one that carries a complete stock of
parts for Bagnabox television sets.  I am
trying to locate a part for a 1975 T.V. unit.

        The television set I want to repair is
a Bagnabox black and white, 1975, Model
Number B559-BA253.  The part I need is the
tuner assembly, part number BA253-TA105.
These numbers came from a circuit diagram
for the T.V. unit.  I am enclosing a copy of
the diagram with this letter.

        Please let me know if you have the part
in stock and how much it costs.  Or you may
send it to me C.O.D. at the above address.
Thank you for your assistance.

                          Very truly yours,

                          Donald O. Lee
                          Donald O. Lee

Enclosure
```

1. The complete address of the writer

2. The date (don't abbreviate it)

3. The inside address (name and address of the reader)

4. The salutation (if you don't know the name, use one of these):
   Dear Sir:
   Dear Madam:
   Gentlemen:

5. The body of the letter (paragraphs)

6. The complimentary close (one of these):
   Sincerely,
   Sincerely yours,
   Yours sincerely,
   Very truly yours,

7. Signature
   a. Name handwritten in ink
   b. Name typed 4 spaces below complimentary close

Business letters should be brief but complete, written in clear and simple language. They should sound friendly unless you have excellent reasons for being angry. The first paragraph should tell the reader briefly what the rest of the letter is about or why you are writing it. The middle paragraphs should tell what you want done. They should give all the information the reader will need in order to do it. The last paragraph should leave the reader with a good feeling and a good impression of you. It may also sum up what you are expecting him or her to do.

Controlled Composition 29.1
Practice Writing a Business Letter to Make a Reservation

Copy the following business letter, making the following changes. Put your own address in the upper right-hand corner (not your name—that goes at the bottom). Use today's date. Change the arrival date to one month from today and the departure date to one week later. Make the reservation for two persons instead of four, at a rate of $40.00 per day. Use your own name and signature in place of the name "A. A. Student." Put a box around each of your changes, proofread, and have your instructor check your paper against the answer key.

597 College Drive
Campusville, CA 93162
May 20, 1980

Happy Hours Resort Hotel
1092 Mission Bay Drive
San Diego, CA 92109

Gentlemen:

Please reserve a room for a party of four (two adults and two children) for the week of June 3 through June 9. We expect to arrive at approximately 7:00 p.m. the evening of June 3 and depart before 11:00 a.m. on June 10.

We will need transportation from and to the San Diego airport. Do you have a limousine service, and, if so, is there any charge for using it?

My check for $70.00 is enclosed to cover deposit required for the first night. Please confirm this reservation as soon as possible. Thank you.

Sincerely yours,

A. A. Student

A. A. Student

Enclosure

Controlled Composition 29.2
Business Letter to Order a Product

Read the following newspaper ad by Personalized Mail Order Company. Then write a letter similar to the one below the ad, but instead of ordering address labels, order the green business cards. Use standard business letter form, today's date, and your own name and address. You may invent the name of your business or use the name of Fee Enterprise Systems, Inc.

PERSONALIZED MAIL ORDER COMPANY
6039 Gumback Lane, Silver Wings, MD 20907

HOW TO ORDER: Write to the above address, stating item(s) desired, quantity wanted, stock number, and dollar amount. Enclose check or money order made payable to PERSONALIZED MAIL ORDER COMPANY, or give your Visa card and handling charges as follows: if order is under $2.00, add $.39; from $2.01 to $5.00, add $1.00; over $5.01, add $2.00. For the personalized printing, print each line as you wish it to appear on your labels or cards.

MULTICOLOR ADDRESS LABELS

1000 labels with cheery designs of red, blue, and green. Your name and return address printed in black on white gummed labels. Any four lines, 25 letters and spaces per line. 2″ long.

AL-1059 Cheery Labels $1.79

DELUXE BUSINESS CARDS

Your name, company, address and phone number printed on fine card stock, 200 per set. Choose gray with black print or green with dark green print, up to 5 lines, 35 letters and spaces per line. Please print.

BC–4128 Gray Bus. Cards $2.98

BC–4129 Green Bus. Cards $2.98

11970 Marine View Dr. S.W.
Seattle, WA 98146
March 15, 1980

Personalized Mail Order Co.
6039 Gumback Lane
Silver Wings, MD 20907

DO NOT WRITE IN THIS BOOK

Gentlemen:

Please send me one set of 1000 labels, Stock Number AL–1059, imprinted with the following name and address:

Ms. Christy Gerhart
1807 N. 82nd
Seattle, WA 98103

You may charge my Visa Card, Number 4019–001–375–5509, in the amount of $1.79 plus .39 postage and handling charge, or a total of $2.18.

Prompt delivery will be appreciated, as I will need the new labels in exactly three weeks.

Sincerely yours,

Christy Gerhart

Christy Gerhart

Creating

29.3   Write a letter to a store or business, complaining about some unsatisfactory service or a product you want to return. Be sure you sound reasonable, not just angry, and give all the information that the business will need in order to satisfy you (that is, tell them exactly what you want them to do about the problem). Use standard business letter form.

29.4   Using standard business letter form, write away for something you have seen in a catalog or newspaper ad. Be sure to give all the information necessary about size, color, model number, and so on, and whether you want it sent c.o.d. or charged to your account.

29.5   Write a letter to the editor of your local newspaper or school newspaper, praising or criticizing something about the community. Mail it in and see if it gets published. Use standard business letter form.

29.6 Write a letter to your representative in the House of Representatives or the Senate telling him or her your views on some issue he or she will soon be voting on. You can get your representative's name and address from your local library.

LESSON
30

Letters of Application and Résumés

If you were an employer, would you be strongly interested in interviewing the person who wrote these letters?

Writer No. 1

Dear Sir:

This letter is to give you the required information for the openings you have for salesmen in your store.

I'm 26 and have five years experience as a salesman. I think I'm the man you need for this position. I want to talk about the salary. I won't accept this position for a salary under $1,000 monthly, and I won't work on Sundays either. I am willing to cooperate with all the company policies.

Very truly yours,

Writer No. 2

Dear Sir:

I am writing about your ad in Monday's Bakersfield paper. You said you need a bookkeeper, and I thought I would check it out. I've had three years of bookkeeping and also other business classes. Please indicate the time for an interview with you.

Yours very truly,

You probably feel that Writer No. 1 is too sure of himself and too demanding before he has had an interview and discovered what the employer can offer. Writer No. 2 doesn't sound very interested in getting a job. Her letter is so unclear we can't tell whether she has had bookkeeping experience or just book-keeping classes. And she seems to be ordering the employer to give her an interview rather than asking him politely for one. She may wonder why she doesn't get one!

Here are some tips for writing a good letter of application:

1. Show interest in the employer's business, together with modest confidence in your own ability. Don't brag, but don't put yourself down.
2. Include enough information, but not too much. Don't tell your whole life history, but tell enough to show you are qualified for the position. Give your address, telephone, and any other information that will make it easy for the employer to contact you.
3. Write well. Use clear, correct sentences and well-organized paragraphs. Choose words that sound courteous, cheerful, and sincere. Make it brief but complete. Proofread your final draft before you mail it because careless errors in writing will make you seem incompetent.
4. Consider the employer's needs, not just your own. Tell him what you can do for him, not what he can do for you. You can use the word *I,* but don't overdo it or you may sound self-centered.
5. Use standard words. Slang is not appropriate in a letter of application, and using too many big words or flowery words can make you sound insincere. Choose frank, businesslike words. Avoid clichés (fixed expressions that have been used over and over, like "eager beaver").
6. Make the appearance attractive. Use standard business letter form (see Lesson 29) on plain white paper of good quality, 8½ × 11 inches in size. Type the letter if possible, or write neatly in ink. Use one side of the paper only. Send only the original, never a carbon copy.
7. Begin and end well. The first paragraph should tell the purpose of the letter and how you learned of the position. It should sound interesting without seeming overstrained. The last paragraph must ask for an interview and tell the employer how to contact you.
8. If you use a résumé (pronounced rez-uh-MAY), send it along with a cover letter. A sample cover letter and résumé are shown on the next two pages.

SAMPLE COVER LETTER

2906 College Avenue
Campusville, CA 95801
May 10, 1980

Fairfield Equipment Company
P. O. Box 216
Campusville, CA 95809

Gentlemen:

Your ad in today's Tribune for a farm equipment sales agent
interests me. Please consider me for the position.

I am familiar with farm equipment and have had experience
operating tractors and harvesters. I grew up on a small farm and
have worked on corporate farms for the past three summers.

My college major is agribusiness, and I expect to graduate in June
of this year. I have also taken some welding courses and can do
minor repairs. Please see the enclosed résumé for further details.

Although I have had no sales experience, my knowledge of farm
practices and equipment should give me valuable background. I am
willing to take whatever training you feel I will need to be successful.

May I have an interview at your convenience? You may reach me
at 449-7526 any weekday after 4:00, or anytime on weekends.

Sincerely yours,

A. A. Student

A. A. Student

Enclosure

SAMPLE RÉSUMÉ

A. A. STUDENT
2906 College Avenue
Campusville, CA 95801
Telephone (916) 449-7526

Date: May 10, 1980
Occupational goals: farm
    management, agribusiness sales,
    consultation, or related work

PERSONAL DATA

Age 21	Height 5'11"
Married, no children	Weight 185 lbs.
Health excellent	No military experience

EDUCATION

1977–1980   Campusville Community College, Campusville, CA 95801
Major in agribusiness, some courses in marketing, bookkeeping, welding, and personnel management. Associate of Arts degree expected in June, 1980.

1973–1977   Student at Alcott High School, Campusville, CA. Served as vice-president of junior class, 1975–1976.

WORK EXPERIENCE

1979 summer   Fabbri Bros. Farms, Wasco, CA
General farm work, harvest of alfalfa and cotton crops

1978 summer   Heywood Farms, Delano, CA
Grape harvesting, payroll, clerical work

1977 summer   Larson's Farms, Oildale, CA
General farm work, care of cattle

ACTIVITIES

Swimming	Campusville Ag Students Club treasurer
Raising dogs	Formerly 4-H Club president

REFERENCES

Mr. Jeff Fabbri	Mr. Harold Heywood
Fabbri Bros. Farms	Heywood Farms, Inc.
P. O. Box 900	P. O. Box 260
Wasco, CA 93280	Delano, CA 93215

Controlled Composition 30.1
Practice Writing a Résumé

Taking whatever details you need from the following story about Phillip Riles, write a résumé with the occupational goal of retail sales manager. Follow the form suggested in Lesson 30.

Information About Phillip Riles

Phillip Riles was born August 1, 1955. He grew up in Salt Lake City, Utah, and graduated from West High School in 1973 with a *C+* average. He played quarterback on his high school football team and served as business manager on the yearbook staff.

In 1973 he moved to California and attended Sacramento City College. From June, 1973, to June, 1975, he worked part-time at Harvey's Shell Station, 4700 Freeport Blvd., Sacramento, CA 95822. He serviced cars, did lube jobs, closed the station by himself at 9:00 P.M. every night, and balanced the daily cash receipts. The station owner, Harvey Johnson, offerred to give him a reference. Phillip graduated from Sacramento City College in June, 1975, with an Associate of Arts degree and a major in psychology.

He married Francine Terry in July, 1975, and moved to 5930—24th St., Sacramento, CA 95822. The couple still live at this address with their son Jason, born October 8, 1978. Their telephone number is (916) 391–8646.

From July, 1975, until now he has worked full-time for Mrs. Adelaide Jenner at Jenner's Department Store, a small retail store in a shopping center at 4520 Freeport Blvd., Sacramento CA 95822. His duties include selling shoes and sporting goods, buying merchandise, stocking shelves, preparing displays, and maintaining inventory records. He feels he has learned as much as his present position can teach him, and he believes he is ready for management responsibilities. He is vice-president of the Southside Businessmen's Association. His hobbies of bowling and swimming help him to keep fit at 175 pounds (he is 5 feet 11 inches tall).

Controlled Composition 30.2
Practice Writing a Letter of Application and Résumé

Below is an example of a well-written letter of application. However, the writer could have chosen to write it in two parts—a short cover letter and an attached résumé giving more details. Pretend you are Jennifer Brown, and rewrite it in that form. The cover letter should tell how you learned of the job, why you want it, and how you are qualified for it (that is, a brief summary of experience or interests related to the work). It should mention that a résumé is enclosed, request an interview, and give a telephone number where you can be easily reached. The résumé should follow the model in Lesson 30.

Proofread carefully; then have your instructor check to see how close you have come to the suggested version in the answer key. Yours does not need to be exactly the same. Make up any details you need to complete it.

597 College Drive
Bakersfield, CA 93305
May 20, 1980

Dr. M. T. Mercer
Box 718
Bakersfield, CA 93301

Dear Dr. Mercer:

In today's Bakersfield Californian, I noticed your advertisement for a medical psychiatric secretary. Please consider me for this part-time position.

I am a graduate of Foothill High School and a freshman at Bakersfield College. In high school I took several business courses and did some clerical work in the attendance office. In college I am taking business and psychology courses. Since my major is psychology and I have had clerical experience, I am very much interested in this job.

During my junior and senior years of high school I worked as a teacher's aide, doing mostly clerical work. I worked for the Boy Scouts of America in the summer of 1978 and the Science Department at Foothill High School in the summer of 1979. I am now working part-time for the Home Economics Department at Bakersfield College. I learned to operate a switchboard and a ten-key adding machine at the Boy Scout office. I can type from 40 to 45 words a minute.

Because I have reached the maximum salary for my present position, I have decided to seek employment with your firm. I have a special interest in the work you are offering and am confident that I can do an outstanding job for you.

Mr. Oliver Hill has permitted me to use his name as a reference. He is chairman of the Science Department at Foothill High School, 871-4302.

May I have a personal interview at your convenience? If you wish to telephone me, my home telephone is 872–5397; my office phone is 395–4319.

Sincerely yours,

Jennifer Brown

Jennifer Brown

Creating

30.3   Write a cover letter suitable for the résumé of Phillip Riles. Follow the advice and example in Lesson 30.

30.4   Pretend you have just graduated from a college or trade school. Write a letter of application to a company you would like to work for, giving details about your training, work experience, and so on, and asking for an interview. Follow all the suggestions in Lesson 30.

30.5   Choose an ad from your newspaper's "Help Wanted" section, and write a letter applying for the job. You may make up some details for this assignment if necessary, but be sure you give all the information requested in the ad. Follow the suggestions in Lesson 30.

DO NOT WRITE IN THIS BOOK

A BRIEF HANDBOOK FOR CORRECTING ERRORS

This section may be used whenever you need special information to correct errors in your writing. For each writing problem, some advice or rules will be given first, then some examples and a drill exercise. You and your teacher can decide whether you need to do the drill.

Not every writing problem can be covered here, of course. But this handbook section will help you with the most common and important problems. You may also need to look up certain rules in a more complete handbook of English. Good dictionaries also contain rules for spelling and punctuation, usually in the back sections. Every good writer should own a dictionary and a handbook and should use them faithfully.

1
Paragraphing

Rule **Write well-developed, unified paragraphs.**

A paragraph is a group of closely related sentences. It begins with an indented line, usually indented about an inch or five typewritten spaces. When the sentences are closely related, they work together to build upon one central idea. The several paragraphs in an essay or article may be compared to rooms in a house. Each room is a little different from the others, and each room has a purpose of its own, but all of them are connected together to serve the larger purpose of making a home for a family. Similarly, each paragraph has its own purpose and main idea, but all of these contribute to the larger idea of the article or essay. Just as rooms have different sizes and arrangements depending on what they are used for, paragraphs have different lengths and patterns depending on their purpose. They can be as short as one sentence (although that is quite unusual) or as long as about 300 words. But usually they are between 100 and 200 words long.

Beginning writers often wonder how long to make their paragraphs. There is no easy answer because length depends on purpose. Very short paragraphs are often used for special purposes such as the introductory or concluding paragraphs of longer essays and articles. Or they may make a transition (bridge) from one subdivision of the article to another. Short paragraphs also occur in direct speech, or dialogue, because a new paragraph begins every time a different person speaks. News articles use short paragraphs, too, usually summing up the main event or point of the story in the first paragraph and giving more details in the following paragraphs. Many business letters are brief enough to need only one or two short paragraphs, and a secretary may prefer two short paragraphs to one long one in a business letter because of the more pleasing appearance on the page. For all these special purposes, short paragraphs may do very well.

Longer paragraphs are needed, however, to describe something fully or to explain something in detail. A *well-developed* paragraph will contain enough details, examples, reasons, or facts to make it convincing. The *topic sentence* is the general statement of what the paragraph is about, or the main idea that ties the details together. The topic sentence may come at the beginning, end, or some other place in the paragraph. Not all paragraphs have a directly stated topic sentence, but all good paragraphs have a main idea that could be put into the form of a topic sentence.

If all the details in the other sentences relate to the topic sentence (or main idea), your paragraph will have *unity,* meaning oneness. On the other hand, if your thoughts seem to ramble or get off the subject, your paragraph may become *disunified.* You must use judgment in deciding what to include in a paragraph and what to leave out or put into another paragraph.

The greatest problem most beginning writers have with paragraphs is that they do not develop them with enough details or examples to support the general statements they have made. You would be wise to look at well-written paragraphs for models. A good illustration of a paragraph developed with many examples is the one by Haim Ginott in Controlled Composition 15.1, "How Teenagers Bug Their Parents." A paragraph developed by reasons is Controlled Composition 2.2, "Nine Reasons for Not Getting Hired." A paragraph developed by explanation is Controlled Composition 11.2, "Refinishing Old Furniture." Also see the Index under "paragraph development" for examples of other types of development used in this book.

2
Finding Subjects and Verbs

Rule Every sentence must have a subject and a verb. In some cases, the subject is understood.

Here the subject is underlined once and the verb twice.

Money talks.	The music died.	Who cares?
This pen leaks.	Our romance ended.	Can everyone hear?

The subject may be "you" understood:

Come in.	Call me.	Go!

Simple sentence kernels, or sentence cores, like those above can be expanded in almost unlimited ways, like this:

1. This ball-point pen leaks badly.

2. This ball-point pen that is supposed to be so wonderful leaks badly whenever it is left lying down for a few hours.

In order to be sure that your sentences are complete and your subjects and verbs agree, you must be able to find the subject and verb of your main clause.

Sometimes it may seem as if they are buried in a huge pile of expansions, or modifiers. If the sentence is short, the easiest way is to find the verb first. A verb is a word or words that can be put into the past, present, and future. It may include helpers like *can, may, have, has, had, is, are, was, were, been.* If you can't put a word or word group into the past, it isn't a verb. When you have found your verb, ask, "Who or what does this?" And that will be your subject, even if it comes after the verb.

Let's try this system on the following sentence.

At the end of the race, there were six joggers left.

Where is the verb? *Race* isn't a verb here, because it is used with *the. Were* is the only word that can be put into past, present, and future *(were, are, will be).* So *were* is our verb. Who or what were left? Joggers were left. So *joggers* is our subject. And because *joggers* is plural, we must use the plural verb *were.* (For one jogger, we would use *was.*)

When the sentence is long and contains many expansions or modifiers, you may need to recognize them in order to disregard them when looking for your sentence core. Prepositional phrases are modifiers that sometimes confuse students because they end with nouns, and students may mistake those nouns for subjects. That mistake is less likely if you find the verb first and then ask, "Who or what does this?" to find the subject. But it will always pay you to recognize prepositional phrases. Here are some examples with the prepositions underlined.

about the house	down the street	on the floor
above the door	during the war	out of the way
across the street	for the people	out the door
after dinner	from a friend	outside the classroom
around noon	in the basket	over the hill
as a favor	in front of the store	since yesterday
as for you	in regard to your note	through the tunnel
at the game	inside the envelope	throughout the day
because of you	in spite of poor health	to my wife
before ten o'clock	instead of cash	together with a check
below the knee	into my room	under the mat
beside the lake	like my brother	up the stairs
between the bookends	near the school	upon my word
beyond my reach	of the people	with my guests
by the sea	off the table	within your rights

To recognize other expansions as modifiers and not your sentence kernel or core, you will need to understand dependent clauses. Lessons 11 and 12 show how these clauses are made.

Briefly, an *independent clause* is a group of words with a subject and verb that can stand alone as a sentence. A *dependent clause* also has a subject and verb, but it has become a modifier or part of a larger sentence. It begins with a joining word that cripples it and makes it dependent, or unable to stand alone. Here are some examples of dependent clauses with the joining word underlined. (Some of these joining words can also be prepositions.)

after she comes	unless it rains
although I tried	until one has loved
as we understand it	when we get rich
as if they cared	whenever you need me
as though we owned it	where we belong
because he is jealous	wherever you go
before we begin	while they are playing
if nothing happens	
in order that we can do this	(a person) who cares
since we met	(a game) which I like
so that we can do this	(an idea) that excites me
that we can win	(a worker) whom I admire
though it took courage	(a writer) whose work I admire

In finding the subject and verb of a long sentence, first mentally mark out the prepositional phrases and dependent clauses. If you own this book, putting light pencil parentheses around these modifiers may help. Let's try that on our sample sentence:

This ball-point pen (that is supposed to be so wonderful) leaks badly (whenever it is left lying down) (for a few hours).

If we ignore the words in parentheses, we are left with *This ball-point pen leaks badly.* Now we can easily find the verb (*leaks* can be put into the past, so it passes the verb test). Who or what leaks? The pen. *Pen* is our subject. *Ball-point* is an adjective telling which pen, but it could be the subject if the sentence read like this: *This ball-point leaks badly.* We must always consider the way words are used in the sentence to know whether they are modifiers or part of the sentence core.

Exercise A. Find the subjects and verbs of the main clause in the sentences below. Underline the subject once and the verb twice. (You may have a compound subject like *Bill and John* or a compound verb like *ate and slept.*) Put parentheses around prepositional phrases and dependent clauses.

1 The employers from San Jose will be interviewing on May 29.

2 Each of us, in a way, is greedy.

3 Whenever we get the chance, my friends and I play poker to relax.

4 Our friendly game of poker is played with matchsticks.

5 Smoking during the game has been prohibited by the players since we began.

6 The men from Bancroft Hall usually beat the men from Eldridge Hall, who haven't had much experience.

7 One member of the group plays with us regularly but never wins.

8 After the game is over, a great thirst comes over all the players.

9 There are cokes in the refrigerator for anyone who wants them.

10 Anyone who wants coffee at that hour makes his own from a jar of instant.

3
Fragments

Rule Avoid ineffective fragments or incomplete sentences in your writing.

If your instructors mark fragments, or incomplete sentences, often in your writing, the first thing you must do is learn to recognize them. Because the most common kind of fragment is a modifier that should be attached to the sentence before it, you may not recognize such a fragment when proofreading your paper from top to bottom. The sense of the previous sentence carries over. But if you proofread backwards, reading aloud the last sentence first, then the next-to-last, and so on, you will be more likely to hear the "incompleteness" of the fragments. Ask yourself, "If someone walked up to me and said just that much, would it make sense?" If your answer is "No, I'm waiting for more to be said," chances are you have a fragment.

Some kinds of fragments are *effective*. Fragments are all right as answers to direct questions or as exclamations like those underlined below:

Does anyone care about saving the snail-darter? Probably not.

Why do I laugh? Because it hurts too much to cry.

How wonderful! Just what I need!

Fragments are also used often in dialogue, or direct speech, to make it sound more like casual talk:

"Looking for something?" the salesclerk asked hopefully. "A gift for your wife, maybe?"

Try to discover which kinds of fragments you are likely to make. Appositive fragments are discussed in Lesson 13. Dependent clause fragments are discussed in Lessons 11 and 12. Fragments created by treating an *-ing* word as a verb are discussed in Lesson 23. The following examples may be corrected by attaching the fragment, which is really a modifier, to the sentence preceding it.

1 The meeting will be on Thursday. Which is the only day everyone can come.

2 This is delicious stew. Like Grandma used to make.

3 Grandma likes to tell stories. About the days when she walked five miles to school.

4 Stories always sound better around a campfire. When the work is done and everyone is relaxing.

5 We need a sales agent with drive. A person who goes after business and doesn't just wait for it.

6 He wandered from country to country. Never being able to call any place "home."

Fragments may also be corrected by adding the missing subject, verb, or verb helper.

7 **Fragment:** The men huddled in the trench. The bombs *exploding* all around them.
   Corrected: The bombs *were exploding* all around them.

8 **Fragment:** Many sportsmen come to Barnstown. Where the fishing is best.
   Corrected: *That's* where the fishing is best.

9 **Fragment:** The children climbed into their bunks. Johnny *taking* the upper one.
   Corrected: Johnny *took* the upper one.

Exercise B. If the following items contain fragments, rewrite them correctly on another sheet. If they are correct, put a *C* after the number.

1 The rummage sale offered many bargains. Among them several items of good jewelry.

2 He went everywhere looking for work. First to the gas stations, then to the drive-ins.

3 Grandma is coming to live with us. Which is fine with me.

4 My uncle comes from Las Vegas. A town famous for entertainment and gambling.

5 My car was dying. The brakes, the shocks, the valves—everything needed repair all at once.

6 The stadium was littered with cans, bottles, and discarded wrappers. A mess if I ever saw one.

7 Willie has become an expert golfer. He is planning to enter some tournaments this spring.

8 The Jensens grow watermelons by the creek. Where they can get lots of water and sunshine.

9 The boy rested on a fallen log. His faithful dog beside him.

10 These workers are picking grapes. Whereas the others are picking cotton.

4

Fused and Comma-Spliced Sentences

Rule Avoid fused sentences and comma-spliced sentences in your writing.

Fused sentences occur when two sentences are put together with no punctuation between them. Comma-spliced sentences occur when two sentences are joined only by a comma. These errors are sometimes called run-on or run-together sentences.

Fused Sentence: I tried to talk to him it didn't do any good.
Comma Splice: I tried to talk to him, it didn't do any good.

There are four ways to correct fused or comma-spliced sentences:

1. Make two sentences, like this:
    I tried to talk to him. It didn't do any good.
2. Make a compound sentence with a semicolon, like this:
    I tried to talk to him; it didn't do any good.
3. Make a compound sentence with a comma and one of these seven joining words: *and, but, or, nor, for, so, yet.* (Also see Lesson 10.)
    I tried to talk to him, *but* it didn't do any good.
4. Subordinate one of the clauses (see Lessons 11 and 12).
    Although I tried to talk to him, it didn't do any good.

To see why these four ways of handling the sentence are all right, whereas the fused sentence and comma-spliced sentence are not, you must know the difference between an *independent clause* (which can stand alone as a sentence) and a *dependent clause* (which cannot stand alone as a sentence). A *clause* is a group of words with a subject and verb. Every sentence must contain at least one independent clause (example: *I tried to talk to him.*) If it contains two or more independent clauses it is a *compound sentence,* as explained in Lesson 10. But the independent clauses must be joined by a semicolon or by a comma and one of these joining words:

DO NOT WRITE IN THIS BOOK

$$\text{independent clause} + \text{comma} + \left\{ \begin{array}{l} \text{and} \\ \text{but} \\ \text{or} \\ \text{nor} \\ \text{for} \\ \text{so} \\ \text{yet} \end{array} \right\} + \text{independent clause}$$

A clause becomes *dependent* (and therefore a modifier, unable to stand alone) when it begins with one of these joining words: *after, although, as, as if, as though, because, before, if, in order that, since, so that, that, though, unless, until, when, whenever, where, while.* Examples of these words in dependent clauses can be seen in Section 2, "Finding Subjects and Verbs." Generally speaking, we do not need any punctuation if we add a dependent clause (modifier) to the end of an independent clause, like this:

(independent)   (dependent)
He wouldn't listen *when* I tried to talk to him.

But if the dependent clause comes first, we signal the reader with a comma where the dependent clause ends and the main clause begins:

(dependent)   (comma)   (independent)
When I tried to talk to him, he wouldn't listen.

Other examples of dependent clauses are given in Lessons 11 and 12.
Do not confuse the following adverbs with joining words: *then, however, therefore, moreover, nevertheless, consequently.* The word *then* is particularly troublesome because it looks like *when,* a true joining word. But these adverbs are not true joining words because they can be moved around in their clauses; they are not fixed at the beginning of the clause. So they cannot make a clause dependent, and a semicolon is still needed between the independent clauses when those adverbs are used.

Exercise C. Correct the following fused and comma-spliced sentences by making either two sentences or a compound sentence out of each.

1 Plan your time carefully then you will get more done.

2 He doesn't write letters very often, however he usually sends a Christmas card.

3 That store is expensive, nevertheless people like to shop there.

4 The rain was falling in a sad, steady drizzle it seemed as if the whole world were crying.

5 She had changed a lot everybody noticed it.

6 This must be your pencil, it isn't mine.

7 The bank closed at three consequently I didn't make a deposit.

8 He played the lead violin, moreover he did a solo.

9 She never told anyone, even her best friends didn't know.

10 When the boat began to drift, Paul began rowing then Larry took his turn.

5
Subject-Verb Agreement

Rule **Use singular verbs with singular subjects. Use plural verbs with plural or compound subjects.**

Do not be confused by modifiers coming between subject and verb, like these: (subjects are underlined once and verbs twice)

Singular subjects:

One of those cakes is enough.

Neither of the boys drives yet.

Each of the students does a term paper.

Plural and compound subjects:

The firefighters from Station A are sending help.

Orange and blue are complementary colors.

The games a child plays teach him the rules of life.

To identify modifiers that might come between subject and verb, see Section 2, "Finding Subjects and Verbs."

When subjects are joined by *or/nor,* they are not compound subjects. The verb should agree with the closer of the two subjects:

Neither the child nor the parents were to blame.

Either the stereo speakers or the television is turned up high.

In sentences beginning with *there is* or *there are,* the subject comes after the verb (don't think of *there* as your subject).

There is a town named "Disco."

There are fifty-two cards in a deck.

Some words may be singular in one sentence and plural in another. Words like *family, committee, group, jury, class, number,* and *team* may be singular when we are thinking about the group as a whole but plural when we are thinking about the individual members of the group. For example:

Singular: My family is important to me.

Plural: The family are scattered over six states.

Singular: The number of gifts wasn't important.

Plural: Quite a number are dissatisfied with this policy.

Usually however, these words (called *collective nouns*) are treated as singular.
The verb should always agree with its subject, not with some other noun in the sentence.

Her graduation gift was two matching suitcases.
(The subject is *gift,* not *suitcases.*)
Casserole dishes are the main thing we eat.
(The subject is *dishes,* not *thing.*)

Exercise D. Choose the correct verb from those in parentheses. Underline the subject once and the verb twice.

1 Each of us (need, needs) love.

2 Do you know if Marian and Betty (do, does) baby-sitting?

3 Neither the apricot tree nor the cherry tree (have, has) bloomed yet.

4 A typewriter and my mother's favorite necklace (was, were) missing.

5 A song of praise and thanksgiving (was, were) offered.

6 (Has, Have) either Mark or the twins been here?

7 No, neither Mark nor the twins (has, have) been here.

8 The people of Cottonfield County (vote, votes) conservatively.

9 There (are, is) no finer neighbors anywhere.

10 There (are, is) good reasons to expect a record crop this year.

6

Verb Tenses and Forms

Rule Use the verb forms of standard English. Do not confuse past tense and past participle forms.

Verbs are complicated, but they are the most important part of English sentences. You may need to memorize the different verb forms, especially if your first language was not English or if you have grown up in a place where a nonstandard dialect is spoken. A dialect is a special language used by the people in a certain region or by a group with a similar cultural background. It is perfectly correct among the speakers, but it may differ from the language used across the country by the majority of English speakers.

Even if you speak a dialect among your friends and family in order to make them comfortable with you, you may want to write in standard English to be understood by many other kinds of people across the United States. If so, you should memorize the standard forms. Then your education will increase the choices you have in language and in life.

In standard English, regular verbs add -ed for the past tense and the past participle. The *past participle* is the form used with the helper verbs *have, has,* and *had* (explained in Lessons 24, 25, and 26). It is also used with the passive voice (explained in Lessons 27 and 28).

Subject Forms	Verb Forms		
	Present	**Past**	**Past Participle**
I, you, we, they	talk	talked	(have) talked
he, she, it	talks	talked	(has) talked

Irregular verbs may use different endings or completely different forms in the past and past participle. The most common irregular verbs are *be, have, do,* and *go.* Here are the principal parts of those verbs.

Subject Form	Verb Forms		
	Present	**Past**	**Past Participle**
I	am	was	(have) been
you, we, they	are	were	(have) been
he, she, it	is	was	(has) been
I, you, we, they	have	had	(have) had
he, she, it	has	had	(has) had
I, you, we, they	do	did	(have) done
he, she, it	does	did	(has) done
I, you, we, they	go	went	(have) gone
he, she, it	goes	went	(has) gone

The irregular verbs *sit, set, lie,* and *lay* often give writers trouble because they look somewhat alike but are used differently. One can *sit* or *lie* down, but he *sets* or *lays* something else down. Examples: I *set* the plant in the window; now it *sits* there. I *lie* down to read, and I *lay* my book beside me. Putting those same sentences into the past tense, we get these: Yesterday I *set* the plant in the window, and it *sat* there. Yesterday I *lay* down to read, and I *laid* my book beside me. The same is true for the verbs *rise* and *raise.* We *rise* by ourselves, and bread *rises* by itself, but we *raise* something else, such as crops, dogs, money, hopes, and so on. Here are the principal parts of these tricky verbs:

Present	**Past**	**Past Participle**
sit	sat	sat
set	set	set
lie	lay	lain
lay	laid	laid
rise	rose	risen
raise	raised	raised

The following irregular verbs are grouped according to patterns so that you can associate those you need to learn with those you already know. In the first column, only one form is given for the present tense—the verb form used with subjects *I, you, we,* and *they.* To use these verbs with *he, she,* or *it,* you would add an *s* (for example, I *become,* he *becomes*).

	Present	**Past**	**Past Participle**
I.	burst	burst	burst
	set	set	set
II.	become	became	become
	come	came	come
	run	ran	run
III.	begin	began	begun
	drink	drank	drunk
	ring	rang	rung
	sing	sang *or* sung	sung
	sink	sank *or* sunk	sunk
	spring	sprang *or* sprung	sprung
	swim	swam	swum

(Note: The past of *sneak* is *sneaked,* not *snuck.*)

	Present	**Past**	**Past Participle**
IV.	blow	blew	blown
	draw	drew	drawn
	fly	flew	flown
	grow	grew	grown
	know	knew	known
	swear	swore	sworn
	tear	tore	torn
	wear	wore	worn
V.	bring	brought	brought
	catch	caught	caught
	dig	dug	dug
	dive	dived *or* dove	dived
	drag	dragged	dragged (not *drug*)
	lead	led	led
	lose	lost	lost
	raise	raised	raised
VI.	arise	arose	arisen
	break	broke	broken
	choose	chose	chosen
	drive	drove	driven
	eat	ate	eaten
	fall	fell	fallen
	forget	forgot	forgotten *or* forgot

forgive	forgave	forgiven
freeze	froze	frozen
get	got	got *or* gotten
give	gave	given
ride	rode	ridden
rise	rose	risen
shake	shook	shaken
shrink	shrank *or* shrunk	shrunk *or* shrunken
speak	spoke	spoken
steal	stole	stolen
take	took	taken
write	wrote	written

Exercise E. Choose the verb form that would be used in standard English.

1 We (was, were) only fooling around.

2 Yesterday I (lay, laid) down to read, and I (lay, laid) my book beside me.

3 We (set up, sat up) thirty chairs so that everyone could (sit, set) down.

4 My teacher has (showed, shown) me several times, but I haven't yet (began, begun) to learn.

5 I (saw, seen) him when he (did, done) it.

6 Since Frank (become, became) an officer, he hasn't (spoke, spoken) to his old friends.

7 My mother (knew, knowed) that the price of beef would (rise, raise) again.

8 He was (shook, shaken) by the experience when his wallet was (stole, stolen).

9 The report has (laid, lain) on his desk all summer; he should have (took, taken) it with him.

10 I (be going, am going) to see if the movie (be, is) that good.

7

Tense Shifts

Rule **If you begin writing a paper in the present tense, do not shift into the past tense unless describing what happened earlier. If you begin writing in the past, do not change suddenly to using the present.**

The problem of shifting in tenses does not usually occur in one sentence. Usually, it takes place in longer papers with some sentences in the present tense and some in the past. The following two sentences will give you an idea what is meant by a tense shift:

> I can see him coming and I'm waiting for him. When he got close, I slugged him.

The shift from the present tense in the first sentence to the past tense in the second one is confusing to the reader.

Sometimes you really need two different tenses, however. For example, you may want to refer to different periods of time, like this:

> Yesterday I *didn't* believe you, but now I *see* I *am* wrong.

It's also all right to use two tenses when part of the sentence is permanently true. We use present tense for statements that are permanently or generally true:

As a teenager, I *learned* that parents *are* human.

You have a choice when you write a story of putting it in the present tense to make it seem as if it is going on right now, or putting it in the past tense. Either of these examples is okay:

1. I *see* the red light flashing. The officer *pulls* me over and *says*, "You in a hurry, Buddy?"
2. I *saw* the red light flashing. The officer *pulled* me over and *said*, "You in a hurry, Buddy?"

But it can be annoying when part of the story is in the present and part in the past, like this:

I *see* the red light flashing. The officer *pulled* me over and *said*, "You in a hurry, Buddy?"

Even if the story is in the past, however, the exact words of a speaker in quotation marks will not necessarily be in the past. They will be exactly what was said.

She *smiled* and *said*, "I *like* you. *Do* you *have* a steady girl?"

More about tenses is explained in Lessons 8 and 9.

Exercise F. These sentences contain shifts in tense. Change the verbs in each example so the tense is the same as in the first verb used.

1 I was just sitting down to watch TV, when suddenly a scared-looking man knocks on the door.

2 I kept hoping the phone would ring, but it never does.

3 I am trying for a job at Marty's, but they said I needed more experience.

4 My mother would be happy if I pick up my shoes and put away my records.

5 In this book the author says that loving yourself was necessary before you could love others.

In the following sentences, change the second verb whenever necessary to keep the time sequence straight. If the sentence is correct, put a *C* beside the number.

6 I was sure that someone has been here.

7 I know now that you were right.

8 The author said that some selfishness is healthy.

9 Joe worked as a gardener last summer and liked it.

10 Huck Finn wanted to be loyal to his friend, so he decides not to turn Jim in.

8

Nouns and Noun Plurals

Rule A noun is the name of a person, place, or thing. Most nouns are made plural by adding *-s* or *-es* (as in *books, speeches*). But some nouns have special plural forms (such as *men, women, children*). In some cases, the end letters change when the noun is made plural (my *life,* their *lives*; one *baby,* two *babies*). The plural of letters and numbers is made with *-'s* (10's, A's).

Here are some plural forms that are not made with *-s*:

man/men	louse/lice	alumnus/alumni
woman/women	mouse/mice	analysis/analyses
child/children	deer/deer	basis/bases
foot/feet	sheep/sheep	crisis/crises
goose/geese	swine/swine	criterion/criteria
tooth/teeth	series/series	medium/media

The words *pants* and *scissors* are always plural. The word *data* is the plural of the Latin word *datum,* but *datum* is seldom used. You should say *these data,* not *this data.*

Never use an apostrophe to make a word plural except in the following cases: letters, numbers, and words that are used as their own names.

Your 4's look like 9's.
I got two *B*'s and three *C*'s this semester.
There are too many *if's, and's,* and *but's* in this contract.

Cases like those above are the only ones in which an apostrophe is used to make a plural. Never use it like this:

Wrong: Give me two ticket's for the Friday night series'.
Right: Give me two tickets for the Friday night series.

See the section on ''Spelling'' for the plurals of words ending in *y* like *baby/babies, body/bodies,* and so on. Check your dictionary for the spelling of plurals you aren't sure of. Look up the word in its base form, and it will give you the plural form as part of the definition.

Exercise G. Choose the correct noun form.

1 My mother is one of the most wonderful (woman, women) I've ever known.

2 Television is a wonderful entertainment (medium, media).

3 The most important (criterion, criteria) for good writing is clarity.

4 He is an (alumnus, alumni) of Harvard University.

5 The hunters didn't kill any (deer, deers) this season.

6 They had the best time of their (lifes, lives).

7 Dr. Ludeke says (mother's, mothers) should nurse their own (babys, babies).

8 Those (junky's, junkies) are abusing their (bodys, bodies) with drugs.

9 Divorce and death are the two greatest (crisis's, crises) any (familys, families) ever have to face.

10 Be sure to dot your (*is, i*'s) and cross your (*ts, t*'s).

9
Pronoun Reference and Agreement

Rule Every pronoun should refer clearly to one antecedent. The *antecedent* is a noun that has been mentioned before, or a general pronoun like *one, anyone, everybody.* The pronoun should agree with its antecedent in sex and number (singular or plural).

In the following examples, pronouns and their antecedents are underlined:

Jerry congratulated herself on the progress of her students.

Does anyone ever really know his own faults, or is he always fooling himself?

The police prided themselves on their arrest record.

If your pronouns could refer to more than one antecedent, your readers may not clearly understand you. Examples:

Debbie told Marilyn that she was in a bad mood.
  (Does *she* refer to Debbie or Marilyn?)
When I soaked my red shirt in hot water, it turned pink.
  (Did the water or the shirt turn pink?)

You might also be misunderstood if your pronouns do not have an antecedent or don't fit the one you intended, like this:

I went to the Broadway, but they didn't have it.

(*They* can't refer to a store, and what is *it*?)

The car ahead doesn't have his headlights on.

(A car has *its* headlights on or a driver has *his* lights on.)

I want to be an actor because I really enjoy it.

(*It* can't refer to *actor*, so *it* has no antecedent. Say, "I enjoy *acting*.")

Another common problem is using vague pronouns like *this, that,* and *which* in such a way that the reader can't tell what they refer to. Examples:

1. I went through all the steps on the first experiment. *This* was repeated on the second one. (*This process* would be clearer; otherwise, the reader may think *this* refers to *experiment*.)
2. My brother borrowed his girl's Barbra Streisand record. Mother doesn't like *that*. (Does *that* refer to the record or the borrowing?)
3. She took the course over because of her low grade, *which* didn't seem fair. (Was the grade unfair, or her having to take the course over? Better: It didn't seem fair that she had to take the course over because of her low grade.)

As mentioned in Lessons 5 and 7, the language is changing regarding the use of *they* and *their* to refer back to singular words like *one, anyone, nobody,* and *someone*. In formal writing, such as college papers and business letters, *he* and *his* are still preferred.

Informal: Someone left *their* books here.
Formal: Someone left *his* books here.
Formal (but slightly awkward): Someone left *his or her* books here.

Remember, too, that *who* refers to persons, *which* to things, and *that* to either persons or things.

It's always best to place your pronouns as near as possible to their antecedents. If the antecedent is so far away that confusion would result, use the noun again instead of a pronoun.

The award for showing the greatest improvement over the year went to newcomer Wendy Williams. It was a trophy. (The pronoun *it* is too far away from *award*. Better to say, "She received a trophy.")

Exercise H. Put a *C* in the blank at the left of any sentence below with clear pronoun reference. Put an *X* if the sentence contains unclear or faulty references, and be prepared to suggest a way of improving it.

_____ **1** I am learning about welding and would like to become one.

_____ **2** I enrolled at Cerro Coso College on June 18, which was a mistake.

_____ **3** Mrs. Gallagher was gracious and polite. This was noticed by everyone.

_____ **4** We don't know anyone who got a refund on their taxes.

_____ **5** In the book it says that blind people do not like being spoken to in a loud voice.

_____ **6** If someone has an accident, the cost of his insurance goes up.

_____ **7** In Mary's budget she allows $100 for clothes.

_____ **8** The company pays well, but they don't have a pension plan.

_____ **9** Anyone who looks outside himself for happiness is unlikely to find it.

_____**10** I'd like your opinion on the class schedule, because it needs changing.

10

Choosing the Right Form of Pronouns and Avoiding Pronoun Shifts

Rule The pronouns *I, we, he, she, they* and *who* are used as subjects. The pronouns *me, us, him, her, them,* and *whom* are used as objects. The pronoun *it* and the pronoun *you* can be either subject or object. Pronouns ending in *-self* or *-selves* are objects.

The sentences below show pronouns properly used.

Subjects: He, she, and I are classmates.
Objects: The noise bothers her, me, and them.
Objects of Prepositions: Karen said goodbye to him and me.

Many people believe wrongly that "he and I" sounds more polite than "him and me," but neither expression is better than the other. They are just used differently. And both can be used in the wrong way:

Wrong: Save a place for he and I.
Right: Save a place for him and me.
Wrong: Him and me are going shopping.
Right: He and I are going shopping.

The easiest way to check such pronoun forms is to pretend that you are using only one of the pronouns at a time, like this:

Save a place for him. (He would sound wrong here.)

Save a place for me. (I would sound wrong here.)

Therefore, write, "Save a place for *him* and *me*." For the same reason, you would say, "*He* is going shopping; *I* am going shopping." Therefore, write, "*He* and *I* are going shopping."

Be especially careful to use *me, us, him, her,* and *them* after prepositions like *to, for, between,* and *against.* A more complete list of prepositions is given in Section 2, "Finding Subjects and Verbs." The examples below are correct:

The fight is just between him and me.

Everyone signed except Jenny and her.

In expressions such as "we girls" or "us boys," choose *we* for subjects and *us* for objects.

We boys have to stick together.

The rules are not fair to us boys.

Do not use *myself* as a substitute for *I* or *me,* or *yourself* as a substitute for *you.*

Weak: I'm fine. How's yourself?

Better: I'm fine. How are you?

Weak: Paul and myself are both in real estate.

Better: Paul and I are both in real estate.

Here are some proper ways to use the *-self* pronouns:

Sometimes I hate myself. They gave themselves a raise. What have you done to yourself? Dennis surprised himself. Connie doesn't take herself too seriously.

Pronoun Shifts

Another problem writers sometimes have with pronouns is shifting back and forth from the *I/me* forms to the *you* forms or *he/she* forms. For example, notice this shift from *I* to *you,* though the writer is talking about the same person:

I love both my parents; it's hard when you have to choose the one you want to live with.

The writer should use either the *you* forms or the *I/me* forms consistently. This problem is more fully discussed in Lessons 6 and 7.

Exercise I. Choose the correct pronoun form.

1 This is Adrienne Bland, saying goodnight from Tom and (I, me).

2 Both Ted and (she, her) are excellent speakers.

3 The idea appeals to both my wife and (I, me).

4 Several of (we, us) students worked in Carter's compaign.

5 Several scholarships were given to (we, us) business majors.

6 The neighbors complained about Jean and (I, me, myself).

7 Louise and (I, me, myself) are forming a car pool.

8 (We, us) voters should be better informed.

9 When his girl complained about his beard, Archie gave (he, him, himself) a shave.

10 Just between you and (I, me, myself), I think that Richard and (she, her) will get married.

11
Spelling Errors

Rule Use standard English spelling. Spelling can be improved by proofreading, memorizing, and applying the rules given below.

Spelling errors are not as important as errors that make writing unclear, but they are the most frequently made errors in student writing. Because employers and others are likely to judge a poor speller as a bad writer, it is well worth your while to learn to spell at least the words you use regularly in your own writing. Unusual words can always be looked up in the dictionary.

Good spelling is also a way of being helpful and courteous to your readers. It gives them the clues they need to pronounce the words they are reading in the same way that you, the writer, would. For example, if you write *then* when you mean *than,* the reader would pronounce the word differently from the way you do. If he finds your writing too confusing, he may give up reading it. So take pride in your spelling in the same way that you take pride in your personal appearance. Make your papers attractive to others and easy for them to read.

Here are the steps you can take to improve your spelling.

1. Get your mind set. Don't label yourself a "poor speller" as if you were born that way and cannot change it. If you have learned a wrong spelling, you can learn a right one. Over 90 percent of English words are written just the way they sound, so don't give up just because of the 10 percent that are tricky. You can learn to spell even difficult words if they are

important to you. After all, don't people with difficult names learn to spell them perfectly?

2. Proofread. Most students really do know how to spell many of the words they miss. Some even copy a correctly spelled word and get it wrong. Get in the habit of looking carefully at what you have written and seeing exactly what letters are there and in what order. Cut out the errors due to carelessness, and you will cut out a great deal of misspelling.

3. Keep a personal spelling list. That is, list all the words you have misspelled in your own writing. If you make a lot of errors, group them into categories of similar mistakes. Categories should include the following: (1) Mistakes due to leaving letters out, such as *fiend* for *friend* or *sophmore* for *sophomore*. (2) Syllables left out, such as *cigrette* for *cigarette* or *particlar* for *particular*. (3) Errors due to mispronunciation, such as *athelete* for *athlete, goverment* for *government,* or *nucular* for *nuclear.* (4) Words that sound alike, such as *our* and *are, passed* and *past* (see the section on "Words Often Confused" in this book). (5) Errors in adding *-ing* and *-ed* endings, such as *writting* for *writing* or *shoped* for *shopped.* (6) Errors in words with *-y* endings, such as *tryed* for *tried* or *bodys* for *bodies.* (7) Errors in using *i-e* combinations, such as *recieve* for *receive* or *beleive* for *believe.* (8) Errors in using apostrophes such as *it's* for *its* or *companys'* for *company's.* (9) Miscellaneous errors, or mistakes with words that don't fit in any of the above categories. By grouping your errors in this way, you may find that most of them can be corrected by learning only a few rules or changing a few habits.

4. Form the habit of breaking long words into syllables. Taking on any big job a little at a time makes it easier. Say each syllable aloud as you write it, giving an exaggerated pronunciation if that helps. For example, *WED-nes-day* instead of the usual pronunciation of "Wensday." Also notice the way long words are built by adding on prefixes at the beginning and suffixes at the end. For example, the word *usual* can add *un* at the beginning and *-ly* at the end, making *unusually.* If you can spell *usual, you* can spell *unusually.* Separating prefixes makes it easier to spell words like *disappear* (dis + appear), *dissatisfied* (dis + satisfied), *unnecessary* (un + necessary), *interracial* (inter + racial) and *misspell* (mis + spell).

5. Memorize effectively. Here is the best way. First, be sure you have the right spelling (no use memorizing a wrong one). If you can't find it in the dictionary, ask your teacher or another good speller. Write the word out carefully five times, saying it aloud as you write it. (Give a special spelling pronunciation, if necessary, for words like *sep-A-rate* or *def-i-NITE.*) Cover up the word, and write it from memory. Then check to be sure you wrote it correctly. Review your personal spelling list often until you can write all the words from memory.

6. Associate tricky words with words you already know. For example, think of *attendance* at a *dance* and you will get the ending right. Contrast *all*

right with *all wrong*. And think of a *compliment* on your *eyes* as being spelled with an *i*. To avoid mixing up *desert* and *dessert*, think of the two *s*'s standing for "sweet stuff." If you make up your own memory devices and associations, you are more likely to remember them.

7. Spelling rules will not help as much as careful proofreading and memorizing because they are mostly concerned with adding suffixes (word endings) like *-ing*, *-ed*, and *-er*. A complete set of spelling rules can be found in a handbook on English, a spelling book, or the back of a good dictionary. Here we list only the most useful ones.

To use the rules, you must know that the vowel letters are *a, e, i, o, u* and sometimes *y*. All other letters are consonants. Some consonant sounds require two letters, such as *th, ph, sh, ch,* and *qu,* and these units should not be separated.

a. *The I-E Rule.* When the sound is like *ee*, then *i* before *e* except after *c*. We turn the *i* and *e* around after *c* because *ci* makes the sound of "sh" in words like *gracious, conscience,* and *social*. In words like *receive* and *ceiling,* we want to make the sound of *cee* and not *shee*. This rule doesn't apply to words like *weigh, friend,* or *science* because they don't contain an *ee* sound. Exceptions are contained in this "nonsense" sentence:

Neither sheik seized either caffeine or protein for the weird leisure of the species.

b. *The Y-to-I Rule.* Change the *y* to *i* when adding a suffix to a word ending in *y* preceded by a consonant. (Examples: *lady/ladies, baby/babies, body/bodies, deny/denies, fry/fries/fried, try/tries/tried.*) This does not apply when the *y* is preceded by a vowel. (Examples: *stay/stayed, boy/boys, valley/valleys.*) But there are a few common exceptions, especially with words that end in *ay*. (Examples: *pay/paid, lay/laid, say/said, day/daily, gay/gaily.*) The Y-to-I Rule does not apply in spelling the plural of proper names. (Examples: *Bradys, Kennedys, Darbys.*)

c. *The Final E Rule.* When we add an *e* to *tap*, it becomes *tape*, and the *a* changes from a short vowel to a name-saying vowel. The same is true for other vowel sounds, as in *pet/Pete, fin/fine, hop/hope,* and *tub/tube*. When we add an ending like *-ed*, *-er*, or *-ing* to a word that ends in *e*, we want to avoid writing *hopeed* or *fineer* because they might be mispronounced as having two syllables *(hop-eed, fin-eer)*. So we drop the final *e* to make words like *taped/taping, competed/competing, fined/fining, writer/writing, hoped/hoping, tubed/tubing*. There is no need to drop the *e* when adding endings like *-ful, -ment,* or *-ly* because that doesn't put two vowels together. So *love + ly = lovely, achieve + ment = achievement, hate + ful = hateful, hope + less = hopeless,* and so on. The *e* is kept in words like *noticeable* and *courageous* to preserve the soft sound of the *c* (like *s*) and the soft sound of *g* (like *j*). When *c* and *g* are followed by *e* and *i*, they are usually pronounced with the soft sounds; but when followed by *a* and *o*, they usually take on the hard sounds (*c* as in *cable*, *g* as in *gone*).

d. *Doubling the Final Consonant Rule.* This rule is related to the one about dropping the final *E*. We need a way to tell the difference between *hop* and *hope* after adding *-ed* or *-ing*. So we double the final consonant letter on *hop* to make *hopped* or *hopping*. Then the *o* keeps the short sound as in *ox*. The same applies to words with other short vowel sounds, like *tapped, petted, bitten, rubbed*.

There is no problem adding endings like *-ed, -er,* and *-ing* when the root word (or base word) ends in two consonants like these: *risk + ed = risked, help + er = helper, thank + ing = thanking, sort + ed = sorted, hunt + er = hunter, string + ing = stringing.*

So when we add endings like *-ed, -er,* and *-ing*, the only words in which we need to double the final consonant are those ending in one consonant letter preceded by one vowel letter, like these:

plan + ed = planned	bar + ed = barred
bed + ing = bedding	put + ing = putting
win + er = winner	spot + er = spotter

Now comes the hard part of the doubling rule. When the root word has more than one syllable, we double the final consonant only if the accent falls on the last syllable, as in these examples:

com-MIT = committed	be-GIN = beginning
re-FER = referred	per-MIT = permitting
con-TROL = controlled	e-QUIP = equipped (Here the *u*
ex-CEL = excelled	goes with the *q;* it is not a vowel sound.)

But we do *not* double the final consonant in words that do not have the accent on the last syllable, like these:

de-VEL-op = developed, developing
LAUN-der = laundered, laundering
BEN-e-fit = benefited, benefiting
ex-HIB-it = exhibited, exhibiting

8. The following list of words most frequently misspelled may help you to make a quick check for correct spellings. But memorizing this list won't help you as much as memorizing your personal spelling list. The words

with a star (*) are often confused with other words that sound something like them. More explanation of these is given in the next section, "Words Often Confused."

accept*
accident
accommodate
accompany
achieve
acquaintance
acquire
across
actually
advice, advise*
affect*
aggressive
all right
amateur
among
amount
apparent
appearance
appreciate
approach
approximate
are (our)*
arguing
argument
arouse
arrangement
article
athlete
athletic
attack
attendance
attitude
author
basically
before
beginner
beginning
believe
benefit

benefited
boundary
business
busy
capital, capitol*
careful
carrying
category
challenge
chief
choose, chose*
clothes, cloths*
coming
comparative
completely
conceiveable
conscience,*
conscious*
consider
consistent
continuous
control
convenience
council, counsel*
criticism
curious
decreased
decision
definitely
denied
dependent
describe
description
desirable
desire
despair
desert, dessert*
difference
disappoint

disastrous
discipline
disease
divide
does, dose*
dominant
doubt
effect, affect*
efficiency
efficient
embarrass
entertain
environment
equipped
especially
exaggerate
excellent
except, accept*
exercise
exist
existence
experience
experiment
familiar
farther, further*
fascinate
favorite
fifty
finally, finely*
financially
foreign
forty
forward
fourth, forth*
friendliness
fulfill
fundamental
further, farther*
government

grammar
guarantee
hear, here*
height
heroes
humorous
ignorant
imagine
immediately
incidentally
independence
intelligence
interest
its, it's*
judgment
knowledge
laborer
later, latter*
leisure
length
license
liveliest
lose, loose*
losing
luxury
maintenance
management
marriage
mathematics
meant
miscellaneous
moral, morale*
naturally
necessary
ninety
occasion
occur, occurred
operate
opinion

opportunity
optimism
our, are*
paid
parallel
particular
passed, past*
peace, piece*
perceive
perform
permanent
personal,
    personnel*
phase
physical
piece, peace*
planned
pleasant
politician
possess
possible
practical
precede
prefer
prejudiced
prepare
prevalent
principal,
    principle*

privilege
probably
proceed
procedure
profession
psychology
pursue
quantity
quiet, quite*
realize
really
recommend
referring
relative
relieve
religion
repetition
represent
resistance
respectfully
response
rhythm
ridiculous
satisfy
scene
schedule
seize
sense
separate

several
shining
significance
similar
sincerely
sophomore
source
speech
sponsor
stake, steak*
strength
studying
subtle
succeed
success
summary
supposed to
surprise
suspense
symbol
technique
temperament
than, then*
their, there,
    they're*
theory
there,
    they're, their*
therefore

they're, their,
    there*
thorough,
    through*
to, too*
together
tragedy
transferred
tries
truly
undoubtedly
used to
using
usually
unusual
vacuum
varies
various
weather,
    whether*
weird
whole
who's, whose*
writing
you're, your*

Exercise J. Fill in the blanks with *i-e* or *e-i* according to the *I-E* rule.

1 ach_____ve	11 fr_____nd	21 rel_____f
2 bel_____ve	12 gr_____f	22 s_____ze
3 br_____f	13 h_____ght	23 rel_____ve
4 c_____ling	14 l_____sure	24 _____ther
5 ch_____f	15 n_____ghbor	25 sh_____k
6 conc_____ted	16 n_____ce	26 th_____f
7 conc_____ve	17 p_____ce	27 w_____gh
8 dec_____ve	18 pr_____st	28 w_____ght
8 f_____ld	19 rec_____ve	29 w_____rd
10 fr_____ght	20 rec_____pt	30 y_____ld

Exercise K. Add the given endings to the base words, keeping or dropping the *e* according to the final-*e* rule.

1 note + ing	**11** hope + ful	**21** excite + ment
2 love + ing	**12** hope + less	**22** stare + ed
3 love + ly	**13** stroke + ed	**23** stare + ing
4 hate + ed	**14** use + ful	**24** face + less
5 hate + ful	**15** use + ing	**25** face + ing
6 like + ing	**16** bite + ing	**26** notice + able
7 like + ly	**17** interfere + ed	**27** courage + ous
8 change + able	**18** shine + ing	**28** bore + ing
9 charge + able	**19** dine + ing	**29** bore + ed
10 hope + ed	**20** write + ing	**30** advantage + ous

Also learn these four exceptions to the rule: *argument, awful, truly,* and *wholly.*

Exercise L. Add the given endings to the base words, following the *Y-to-I* rule and its exceptions.

1 try + s	**8** lady + s	**15** worry + ed	**22** pay + ed
2 try + ed	**9** fry + ed	**16** Colby + s	**23** annoy + ed
3 fly + s	**10** reply + ed	**17** baby + s	**24** salary + s
4 study + s	**11** say + ed	**18** Cassidy + s	**25** carry + ed
5 study + ed	**12** deny + s	**19** attorney + s	**26** body + s
6 day + s	**13** lay + ed	**20** country + s	**27** company + s
7 day + ly	**14** valley + s	**21** dry + s	**28** fry + s

Exercise M. Add the given endings to the base words. Double the final consonant only if (1) the base word ends in a single consonant preceded by a single vowel, (2) the accent falls on the last or only syllable, and (3) the added ending begins with a vowel.

1 begin + ing	**9** refer + ed	**17** firm + er
2 come + ing	**10** drop + ed	**18** offer + ing
3 equip + ed	**11** droop + ed	**19** hate + ing
4 retire + ment	**12** red + ish	**20** stop + ed
5 rot + ing	**13** red + ness	**21** stoop + ed
6 sin + er	**14** bite + ing	**22** unforget + able
7 dine + ing	**15** bit + en	**23** excel + ed
8 big + est	**16** submit + ing	**24** time + ly

12
Words Often Confused

Many words sound alike but are spelled differently when they are used differently. That's why you should always read the definition of a word when you look up the spelling in the dictionary. The spelling could be right for some other meaning but not for the meaning you had in mind. Here are some of the most commonly confused words.

accept, except. To *accept* (verb) is to receive willingly. *Except* (preposition) means to leave out. Good friends *accept* our faults. He'll eat anything *except* turnips. (Note: in a few cases *except* can be a verb meaning to leave out, but most people will not need to use it that way.)

advice, advise. To *advise* (verb) means to give *advice* (noun). *Advise* rhymes with *prize*; *advice* rhymes with *nice*. My lawyer *advised* me to sue. I will follow your *advice*.

affect, effect. To *affect* (verb) means to influence or change something. An *effect* (noun) is a result. In a less common use, *effect* (verb) means to bring into being. Absence will surely *affect* your grade. The *effect* of the drug had worn off. It took six weeks to *effect* the change in our marketing plans.

all ready, already. *Already* (adverb) means before this time. *All ready* (adjective) means the same as *ready*. He's *already* finished. It's winter *already*. He's *all ready* to begin. The report is *all ready*.

angel, angle. An *angel* (pronounced AIN-jel) is a heavenly being. An *angle* (pronounced ANG-gull) is two lines leading away from one point. She sings like an *angel*. The car went off at an *angle*.

are, our. *Are* (verb) is the plural of *am* and *is*. *Our* (pronoun) means belonging to us. We *are* citizens. *Our* house is close to your house.

bath, bathe. To *bathe* (verb) is to take a *bath* (noun) in water. *Bathe* is pronounced with *a* as in *day* and *th* as in *the*.

brake, break. A *brake* (noun) will stop a car or bicycle. We *break* (verb) something into pieces. The car needs new *brakes*. Don't *break* the dish.

breath, breathe. *Breath* (noun) means air taken in; it rhymes with *death*. *Breathe* (verb) means to draw air in; it has an *ee* sound and *th* as in *the*. Take a deep *breath*. *Breathe* deeply.

capital, capitol. A *capitol* (noun) is a building (let the *o* remind you of a dome). A *capital* city (adjective) is the head city, and *capital* punishment is cutting off the head. Also, we use *capital* (a large sum of money) to invest in a business.

choose, chose. *Choose* (verb) rhymes with *booze*. *Chose* is the past of *choose; chose* rhymes with *froze*. I *choose* a partner today. I *chose* a partner yesterday.

clothes, cloths. *Clothes* are what we wear. *Cloths* (rhyming with *moths*) are pieces of material. Hang your *clothes* in the closet. Use these *cloths* to wash the dishes.

coarse, course. *Coarse* (adjective) means rough. We take a *course* in college. His manners were *coarse*. An English *course* is required, of *course*.

compliment, complement. A *compliment* is praise. A *complement* is something that completes. A *compliment* on your eyes is spelled with an *i*. History 17B will *complement* History 17A.

conscience, conscious. A *conscience* (noun) tells right from wrong. To be *conscious* (adjective) is to be awake or aware. My *conscience* bothers me if I tell a lie. I became *conscious* that I have talent.

council, counsel. A *council* (noun) is a group of people or a meeting. To *counsel* (verb) is to give advice. The student *council* meets every week. Please *counsel* me on what courses to take.

desert, dessert. *Dessert* (noun) means "sweet stuff," and so it has two *s*'s. A *desert* (noun) is a barren land. To *desert* (verb) a child is to leave him permanently. (The noun *dessert* and the verb *desert* are pronounced alike.)

do, due. To *do* (verb) is to perform. *Due* (adjective) means owing. *Due to* means because of. Can you *do* this job? These bills are *due* April 1. Shipments were delayed *due to* the floods.

does, dose. *Does* (verb) is a form of *do*. A *dose* is an amount of medicine or drugs. He *does* his job well. Take a *dose* of aspirin at bedtime.

farther, further. *Farther* tells distance. Use *further* for other meanings. How many miles *farther* is it? I have nothing *further* to say.

finally, finely. *Finally* means at the end. *Finely* tells how small or precise something is made. I *finally* finished my work. Add *finely* chopped onion. This violin is a *finely* tuned instrument.

forth, fourth. *Fourth* is the number after *third*. *Forth* means forward. She was in *fourth* place. She drove thirty miles back and *forth* to work.

hear, here. We *hear* with our ears. *Here* is the opposite of *there*. Did you *hear* the Groupies when they were *here*?

its, it's. *It's* is a contraction for *it is* or *it has*. *Its* means belonging to it. *It's* a pleasure to see you again. *It's* been a long time. This book has a spot on *its* cover.

later, latter. *Later* (adverb) means after a certain time. *Latter* (adjective) means the last item mentioned. I'll see you *later*. Of those two poems, the *latter* is more famous.

lead, led. *Lead* (verb) rhymes with *seed*; the past tense of *lead* is *led*. *Lead* (noun) rhymes with *bed*; it is a metal. We expect a leader to *lead*. Last year some students were *led* into trouble. Use a *lead* pencil.

loose, lose. *Loose* means not tight; it rhymes with *goose*. If you *lose* something, you don't keep it; *lose* rhymes with *shoes*. The goose got *loose*. Did you *lose* your shoes?

maybe, may be. *Maybe* means perhaps. *May be* means might be. *Maybe* I'll have some spare time. You *may be* right.

moral, morale. *Moral* is pronounced MOR-al; it relates to righteousness. *Morale* is pronounced mor-AL; it relates to spirit. Power can be used for *moral* or immoral purposes. The team has a high *morale*.

passed, past. *Passed* (verb) is a form of *pass*. Use *past* for all other meanings. I *passed* the course. The players *passed* the ball. Let's not talk about the *past*. We need your *past* employment record. She walked right *past* me. It's *past* forgetting.

patience, patients. *Patience* is calm endurance. *Patients* are people doctors and nurses care for. My mother has lots of *patience* with children. The nurse was devoted to her *patients*.

peace, piece. *Peace* means calmness. *Piece* is a part of a whole. The minister's words brought me great *peace*. I'd like a *piece* of pie.

personal, personnel. *Personal* is pronounced PURS-on-al; it means belonging to or relating to a person. *Personnel* is pronounced per-son-NEL; it means workers. A purse is *personal* property. Mr. Nell is the *personnel* manager.

principal, principle. *Principal* means *main*; both words have an *a* in them. A *principle* is a *rule*; both words end in *le*. The *principal* is the main leader in a school. My *principal* occupation is my main occupation. The bank pays interest on the *principal*, or main amount of money. I live according to high *principles* (rules). I dislike gambling on *principle* (a rule of conduct).

quiet, quite. *Quiet* rhymes with DI-et; it means not noisy. *Quite* rhymes with *bite;* it means very. The library is a *quiet* place. The marriage seems *quite* happy. I'm not *quite* ready.

sense, since. *Sense* rhymes with *cents;* it means meaning. *Since* rhymes with *mince;* it means because, or after a certain time. That speaker didn't make *sense.* I've been up *since* 5:00 A.M. *Since* you asked, I'll tell you.

than, then. *Than* compares things; it rhymes with *man. Then* refers to time; it rhymes with *men.* I like beef better *than* chicken. Read the lesson and *then* answer the questions.

their, there, they're. *Their* means belonging to them. *They're* is a contraction for *they are. There* is the opposite of *here* (compare the spelling of *here* and *there). There* is also an introductory word. *They're* taking *their* friends over *there. There* is a basketball game tonight.

thorough, through. *Thorough* is pronounced THOR-oh; it means complete. *Through* is pronounced like *threw;* it means in one end and out the other. He did a *thorough* job. They went *through* the tunnel. He hasn't been *through* high school.

to, too, two. *Two* is a number. *Too* means also or more than enough. *To* is used for all other meanings. (*Hint:* If you can shorten the sound to just *t,* you are using *to,* not *too.* Example: going t' town t' shop.) I want *two* children. Are you a Leo, *too?* These pants are *too* short. We went *to* the city *to* shop.

weather, whether. *Weather* refers to outdoor conditions like rain. *Whether* is used for choices; you should pronounce the *wh* as in *where.* The *weather* was warm and sunny. I don't know *whether* to take that job or not.

whose, who's. *Whose* means belonging to whom. *Who's* is a contraction of *who is* or *who has. Whose* records are those? *Who's* that girl? Guess *who's* been here.

Exercise N. Choose the correct words from the choices in parentheses.

1 (Your, you're) very gracious to (except, accept) my apology.

2 The lawyer's (advice, advise) didn't (affect, effect) my decision.

3 Marian is buying new (cloths, clothes) because (its, it's) Easter.

4 My mother (past, passed) away during the (past, passed) year.

5 Life is (to, too) lonely (since, sense) you left.

6 The cheerleaders got us (already, all ready) and (lead, led) us in a cheer.

7 The nurse seemed like an (angel, angle) to her (patients, patience).

8 My bills are (do, due), but I can (chose, choose) to pay only part of them now.

9 Don't give them (desert, dessert) because (their, they're) on a diet.

10 I don't know (weather, whether) I can sleep in such a (quiet, quite) room.

13
Adverb-Adjective Confusion

Rule Use adjectives to describe nouns. Use adverbs to tell how something is done. Do not confuse adjective and adverb forms.

Here is simple way to tell whether the word you are using is an adjective. Put it in both slots of this pattern:

That _____ person (or thing) is very _____ .

Examples: That *boring* person is very *boring*. That *ugly* frog is very *ugly*. Adverbs tell where, when, and how, but the ones most likely to be confused with adjectives are those that tell how something is done. These adverbs are correctly used:

He did the job *well, quickly,* and *carefully.*
Those colors go together *well.*

Use *good* and *bad* as adjectives; use *well* and *badly* as adverbs:

She did a *good* job. She did it *well.*
She did a *bad* job. She did it *badly.*

Adjectives—not adverbs—often follow verbs like *be, seem, appear, become,* and the verbs of the senses like *taste, smell, sound, look,* and *feel.* (You may have heard these verbs called *linking verbs.*) Examples:

I feel *bad.* That sounds *good.* It smells *awful.* It tastes *delicious.*
You seem *unhappy.* He became *famous.* She appears *intelligent.*
They will be *sorry.* That is *impossible.*

Although many adverbs end in *-ly,* not all of them do. A few words like *fast* can be either adjectives or adverbs depending on how they are used:

He bought a *fast* car (adj.) and drove it *fast* (adv.)
It was a *hard* job (adj.) and they worked *hard* (adv.)

However, the word *real* should be used only as an adjective. The adverb form is *really,* which often comes before another adverb or adjective.

The coat was *real* leather. It looked *really* nice.
The commercial was *really* well done.

Exercise O. Choose the correct adjective or adverb form.

1 I feel (bad, badly) about forgetting your birthday.

2 That color looks (good, well) on you.

3 The movie was in (bad, badly) taste, and the actors performed (bad, badly).

4 The chair was made so (good, well) that it lasted forty years.

5 He wanted to win (real bad, really bad, really badly).

6 This watch runs (good, well); it keeps (good, well) time.

7 Grandma said it was unpatriotic when Grandpa sang the national anthem so (bad, badly).

8 This tie goes (good, well) with that suit.

9 The glue on the envelopes tasted (horrible, horribly).

10 Shoplifters usually dress (good, well) because if they appear (wealthy, wealthily), they will seem unlikely to steal.

14

Contractions and Possessive Forms

Rule Form contractions with an apostrophe (') where the letters have been left out.

Rule Do not use apostrophes with possessive pronouns, but use them with possessive nouns.

Contractions come from speech habits of sliding words together, such as *isn't* for *is not.* Writing imitates this slurred pronunciation by putting the two words together and placing an apostrophe where a letter or letters have been left out. Here are some examples:

is not = isn't	I am = I'm	I have (been) = I've been
are not = aren't	you are = you're	you have (been) = you've been
does not = doesn't	he is = he's	he has (been) = he's been
do not = don't	it is = it's	it has (been) = it's been
will not = won't*	we are = we're	we have (been) = we've been
have not = haven't	they are = they're	they have (been) = they've been
cannot = can't	who is = who's	who has (been) = who's been

* The contraction for *will not* changes some letters (to *won't*) as well as adding an apostrophe. The contraction for *am not* also changes letters (to *ain't*), but *ain't* is frowned upon in most sections of the United States. It should not be used in standard English.

should not = shouldn't	I would = I'd	should have = should've**
would not = wouldn't	they would = they'd	would have = would've**
there is = there's	he would = he'd	let us = let's
where is = where's	he will = he'll	I will = I'll

The contractions *you're, it's, they're* and *who's* all stand in place of two words (*you are, it is,* and so on). They should never be confused with the pronouns *your, its, their,* and *whose.* These are special forms that show ownership or possession, like *his, her, my, our, hers, mine, ours, yours,* and *theirs.* None of these possessive pronouns use apostrophes:

Whose house are we going to? *Their* house.
Her house has its charm, but *my* house is cozier.
Whose idea did you like best—*mine, his,* or *hers?*

Because they have these special forms, personal pronouns do not need apostrophes to show possession. They are already possessive. But nouns cannot have special forms to show possession because there are too many nouns. So we use apostrophes with nouns to show ownership. We also add an *-s* to show ownership unless the noun already ends in *s.* Pronouns ending with *one* or *body* are treated like nouns. Here are some examples:

Bruce's wife	a city's parks
Bill Smith's garden	a country's problems
my mother's request	a company's records
the dog's dish	the women's department
anybody's guess	the children's playground
someone's idea	nobody's fault

If the noun already ends in *s,* we need only an apostrophe to show ownership:

Moses' tables	two cities' parks
the Smiths' house	two countries' problems
two mothers' concerns	two companies' records
two boys' lockers	two families' quarrels
the girls' gym	ladies' restroom
our pets' dishes	two babies' clothes

Occasionally we add -'s to words ending in s if the second s sound would probably be pronounced:

the boss's desk   the Harris's party   Chris's brother.

** Never write *should of* for *should've,* or *would of* for *would've.*

We show that something belongs to a certain time by using apostrophes:

a day's work   an hour's pay   Saturday's game   today's special

Apostrophes and Plurals

In most cases, you would be wrong to use an apostrophe just to make a word plural. In the following example, the nouns are *not* possessive, only plural, and would not need any apostrophe:

I know the *Smiths.* They own two *bakeries.*

However, we do use apostrophes to make letters and numbers plural. See the handbook section entitled "Nouns and Noun Plurals."

Exercise P. Choose the correct form of contraction or pronoun.

1 You (should've, should of) gone to the (Jones's, Jone's) party.

2 (Whose, Who's) purse was left in the (lady's, ladies') room?

3 (Whose, Who's) going to Friday (night's, nights') game with the (Bradshaws, Bradshaw's)?

4 (It's, Its) clear that all the (students, student's) understand (their, they're) fractions.

5 (Their, They're) giving a (days, day's) pay to the (childrens', children's) home.

6 (It's, Its) not true that every dog has (it's, its) day.

7 You (should've, should of) known that (your, you're) liked by all (your, you're) teachers.

8 Those two (countries, country's) are always fighting over (their, they're) boundaries and (their, they're) never going to stop.

9 It's (anyone's, anyones') guess (whose, who's) play will win in the (city's, citys') contest.

10 The (secretaries, secretary's) played a joke by switching the photographs on (their, they're) (boss's, bosses') desks.

11 I never (would've, would of) guessed that Agatha (Smith's, Smiths) play would have the long run (it's, its) had.

12 In (its, it's) earlier arrangement, that (Beatles', Beatle's) song was a favorite of (our's, ours).

15

Commas to Separate

Rule 1 Use a comma between independent clauses if they are joined by *and, but, or, nor, for, so, yet.*

Rule 2 Use a comma after an introductory adverbial clause or phrase.

Rule 3 Use commas to separate items in a series.

Commas are a useful tool for you and your readers. Just as pauses in speech help those who are listening, commas help your readers by showing them how words are grouped together in your sentences and separated from other groups of words. In the sentences below, for example, commas help to separate clauses. The longer your sentences are, the more important such separations become:

1. He and his children argued and fought constantly and bitterly, and the children left home as soon as they were old enough.
2. After the children left, his home was peaceful but strangely empty.

In the examples above, *and* joins subjects, verbs, and modifiers as well as clauses; *but* joins the adjectives *peaceful* and *empty.* Because these joining words can join not only clauses but also single words and short phrases, the comma between clauses helps the reader to separate the major ideas (main clauses) from less important modifying ideas within those clauses. In the second example, the comma signals the reader that the dependent clause (modifier clause) is ending and the main clause is beginning. Without the comma after *left,* the reader might group the words like this:

After the children left his home . . .

Then the rest of the sentence would be unclear, and the reader would have to go back, reread the sentence, and try to guess how to group the clauses so that they make sense. A good writer helps his readers by taking the guesswork out as much as possible. More about clauses and their punctuation is explained in Lessons 10, 11, and 12.

Commas are also used to separate items in a series, like these:

Everything I like is illegal, sinful, fattening, or cancer-causing. (a series of adjectives)
I'd go through fire, under water, and across a freeway to be with you. (a series of prepositional phrases)

Sometimes the comma is omitted before *and* at the end of a series, but more often it is used.

Some adjectives in a series have been used together so much that they seem like one unit and don't require commas:

a dear little old lady   a funny old Irish gentleman
a nice little boy   a run-down old building

To decide whether you need commas or whether you are using a fixed phrase like those above, see if the adjectives would sound right in a different order. In the examples below, the adjectives sound so unusual that it is clear they should be put back into normal fixed order and do not require commas.

an old little dear lady   an Irish old funny gentleman

However, if the adjectives do sound all right in a different order, they will require commas if there are two or more:

1. Everything I like is fattening, cancer-causing, sinful, or illegal.
2. He was surrounded by an angry, ugly mob.

Items in a series are explained further in Lesson 15.

Exercise Q. Insert commas as needed according to rules 1, 2, and 3. Do not use any unnecessary commas.

1 When final exams are over in May we head for the beach.

2 The air is blue the water is cool and the gulls are everywhere.

3 Gulls look so lazy in the sky but their lives are a constant struggle for food.

4 In case they fly over your head should be covered.

5 I love the feel of the warm sand and the sun soothes away my cares.

6 The people on a beach come in assorted sizes shapes and colors and they all have different reasons for being there.

7 Some like to get close to nature some are looking for exercise some are avoiding any exercise and some are showing off their beautiful bodies.

8 Every beach has a battered old ice-cream stand surrounded by tired frustrated mothers and their bratty little kids.

9 In spite of the confusion all around us we manage to feel relaxed.

10 We are hooked by the sun and the sand and we hate going back to smog cement and traffic lights.

DO NOT WRITE IN THIS BOOK

16
Commas to Enclose

Rule 4 Use two commas to enclose sentence interrupters.

Rule 5 Enclose nonessential material (sometimes called nonrestrictive) in commas. (If the nonessential material begins or ends a sentence, only one comma is needed.)

Sentence interrupters are extra words or phrases inserted into a statement that would be clear without them. Here are some examples:

Nobody, *I am sure,* would want bad schools.
It is there, *no doubt,* that we made our first mistake.
We lost money but, *to tell the truth,* I'm not sorry.

In writing direct speech or dialogue, we treat expressions like *he said* and *she replied* as interrupters (see also Lesson 20).

"I'm here," *he said,* "if you need me."

As explained in Lessons 12 and 13, appositives and adjective clauses give information that is often interesting and important. But if it is not needed to identify fully the nouns described, it is treated as extra information that requires extra commas.

212

The Proudfit Company, *your neighborhood appliance store*, services what it sells.

Professor Kessler, *who specializes in modern religions*, has been studying cults in the United States.

In the above examples, the nouns were fully identified by name. In the examples below, however, the nouns *company, brother,* and *charts* are not fully identified without the appositive or adjective clause that follows. Therefore, commas are not used.

The company *that sells this TV* also makes repairs.

My brother *Mo* is the oldest son in the family.

This report includes charts *which aren't necessary.*

For additional explanation and examples, see Lessons 12 and 13.

Exercise R. Use commas to enclose sentence interrupters and nonessential material in the sentences below. Do not use unnecessary commas.

1. The local newspaper as a matter of fact has been losing subscribers.

2 A kleptomaniac is a person who helps himself because he can't help himself.

3 They arrested Carl Lightfingers who is a kleptomaniac for shoplifting in a local store.

4 Shoplifting according to our lawyers is a crime which can be punished by imprisonment.

5 Carl's mother an unhappy woman if I ever saw one paid the fine.

6 Would you recommend the company that sold you your television set?

7 I would recommend the Proudfit Company which has given me excellent service.

8 The typists who did the report have been especially careful I believe in making the charts and tables.

9 My favorite city Denver is high in the Rocky Mountains.

10 I am grateful to Randy Dickson who headed my campaign and to all the dedicated workers who helped him.

17

Commas in Dates, Addresses, Direct Address, and Contrasts

DO NOT WRITE IN THIS BOOK

Rule 6 Use a comma after every item in dates and addresses if there is more than one item.

Rule 7 Enclose with commas the name of a person being directly spoken to or words used in place of such a person's name.

Rule 8 Use commas to set off sharp contrasts.

Rule 9 Expressions like *yes, no, oh,* and *well* are followed by commas.

Here are some examples of the uses for commas mentioned in the above rules:

Dates: The meeting was held Friday, September 28, 1979, at 3:00 P.M.
Addresses: You may reach me at 1266 Bryan Avenue, Visalia, CA 93277.
(The zip code is not separated from the state by a comma.)
He was born in El Paso, Texas, in 1960.
Person Spoken To: Thank you, Mr. Bryson, for your help.
Goodbye, friends, and good luck to you.
Contrast: It was Milton, not Shakespeare, who wrote that line.

Other Expressions: Yes, I am free tomorrow.
No, we don't agree with you.
Oh, it's you.
Well, it's about time!

Exercise S. Insert commas as needed according to rules 6, 7, 8, and 9. Do not use unnecessary commas.

1 Yes I am a resident of Tulsa Oklahoma.

2 I have lived in Phoenix Arizona since July 1971.

3 Oh no my name is Johnston not Johnson.

4 Florence was born in Boise Idaho on October 8 1940.

5 The publisher's address is 383 Madison Avenue New York NY 10017.

6 Yes we can get reservations for July 6 at the Green Tree Hotel in Dallas Texas.

7 You're a man if you can raise a baby not just make one.

8 Well are you satisfied now?

9 Do you want our friendship or just our money?

10 I will be in London England on August 19 and in Paris France on September 7.

DO NOT WRITE IN THIS BOOK

18
Capital Letters

Rule Use capital letters as in the examples below. Do not use unnecessary capitals.

Capitalize:

1. The first word of every sentence, including a quoted sentence within another sentence.

   She said, "Flattery will get you anywhere."

2. The first, last, and all important words in a title.

   The Old Man and the Sea   "A Rose for Emily"
   For Whom the Bell Tolls   "Words to Live By"

3. Names of people, places, languages, nationalities, major periods of history, and sacred names.

   Doctor Dorothy Bray   Chicano   the Far East
   Reverend Ted Webb   Puerto Rico   the Middle Ages
   Detroit, Michigan   English   the Savior

4. Names of days of the week, holidays, and months, but not of seasons.

Monday	Christmas	spring
Easter	February	summer

5. A word that replaces a person's name, but not one that just shows a relationship. (Note: if words like *my, a,* and *the* come before such a name, a capital is not used.)

Are you tired, Dear?	Sally is a dear.
It's for you, Dad.	My dad is a carpenter.
Get Mother a chair.	Get your mother a chair.
Where's Uncle Ted?	Ted Phipps is her uncle.

6. Names of particular people, things, or companies, but not general ones.

Particular	**General**
He works for Gulf Oil Company.	He works for an oil company.
Report to Captain Carver.	He's a captain in the army.
Tom joined the U.S. Navy.	We need a strong navy.
Meet me on Bell Street.	What street is this?
He goes to Lane College.	This is a two-year college.
He is taking History 101.	He is taking history and math.
The speech is in the Byrd Building.	The speech is in this building.
Has Doctor Hall seen your throat?	Have you seen a doctor?
The Art Department is small.	In this department, we teach art.
He drives a Toyota.	He drives a foreign car.
They attend First Christian Church.	They attend church often.

Exercise T. Supply capital letters where needed below. Do not use unnecessary capital letters.

1 clifton beverly was born in boston on november 15.

2 if not in september, come later in the fall.

3 the english department will meet tuesday in the library.

4 jane read mutiny on the bounty last summer.

5 does your company have a service department?

6 i am taking economics 10 and spanish 1 next fall.

7 everyone should have math and english skills.

8 the wilson electronics corporation has agencies in sweden and other foreign countries.

9 religions of the far east, including buddhism and hinduism, have many american followers.

10 the romans worshiped several gods and goddesses, including ceres, from whose name the word *cereal* is derived.

19

Periods, Question Marks, Exclamation Marks

Rule End statements with periods, questions with question marks, and expressions of strong emotion with exclamation marks. Don't overuse exclamation marks.

The following examples are correctly punctuated.

> We won**!** Isn't that great**?**
> What**!** You here again**?**
> How romantic**!**

Reading aloud gives you clues about end punctuation. Exclamations are said more forcefully than other speech. Your voice drops where a period goes, and it usually goes up at the end of a question. Exceptions are questions beginning with *who, where, when, why,* and *what;* in these cases, the voice drops at the end. Careful proofreading helps, too, because most students know how to use these marks. They just leave them out carelessly sometimes.

Don't overuse exclamation marks like this:

> I'm coming home**!** It will be good to see you**!!**
> Meet me at the airport Thursday at 8 P.M.**!**

Too much emphasis results in no emphasis at all. So use emphatic marks sparingly, and leave them out if you aren't sure you need them.

20

Semicolons, Colons, Parentheses, Dashes

Rule **Use special punctuation marks according to standard practice.**

If you learn a few simple uses for special punctuation, you will not need to guess wildly or use punctuation marks that don't fit your purposes. Know which ones to use in what situations, and don't use any punctuation marks without a reason for doing so.

Rule 1 **Use a semicolon (;) between independent clauses in a compound sentence. (Also see Lesson 10 about compound sentences.)**

He came; he saw; he conquered.

Rule 2 **Use a colon (:) after a complete statement when a list, long quotation, or explanation follows.**

Colon: These are the things I like best: music, dance, and theater.
No Colon: I like music, dance, and theater. (No colon because "I like" is not a complete statement.)
Colon: Please give me the following information: birthdate, address, and telephone number.
No Colon: The information we need is your birthdate, address, and telephone number.

Rule 3 **Use parentheses (like this) to enclose sentence interrupters that aren't very important. Use dashes—like this—to enclose sentence interrupters that you want to emphasize.**

Like the exclamation mark, dashes should not be overused. *Never* use a dash as a substitute for a period or a semicolon. Parentheses and dashes are especially useful to enclose a sentence interrupter that has commas inside it. (See Lesson 13 for further examples.)

Three precious rights—life, liberty, and the pursuit of happiness—are guaranteed by the constitution.
Horses are quadrupeds (that is, four-footed animals).

Rule 4 **A dash may also be used to set off a final appositive, like this:**

His mind held only one thought—revenge.

Exercise U. Use the appropriate punctuation in the sentences below (question marks, exclamation marks, semicolons, colons, parentheses, and dashes).

1 They gave a great and I mean great performance.

2 If you know three languages Spanish, English, and French you can easily tour the world.

3 When you go camping, don't forget the following items soap, bandages, iodine, and matches.

4 Where does she get the time, patience, and money to paint with oils.

5 To paint with oils you will need three things time, patience, and money.

6 The newspaper reported that a suspect had been arrested however it didn't give his name.

7 How could he do such a thing. It's disgusting.

8 Many words that end in *-ly* are adverbs for example, *slowly,* but some are adjectives for example, *lovely.*

9 The following words are often confused *affect* and *effect, does* and *dose.*

10 Why do so many students confuse the words *their, there,* and *they're.* How careless of them.

21

Quotation Marks, Italics, and Titles

Rule Do not put quotation marks or underlining on your own titles at the top of your papers, but if you refer to other titles in your writing, use quotation marks or underlining to separate them from your words.

Use quotation marks around the name of a song, story, poem, essay, or other short work. Use underlining for the names of longer works such as books, newspapers, and magazines. Underlining means the words would be italicized in print (that is, put in slanted print). Titles of plays and movies may be underlined, but many writers now use quotation marks for titles of plays, movies, and television shows. Here are some examples:

He sang the song "Without a Song."
Stephen Crane's story "The Open Boat" is reprinted in *Best Short Stories*.
Do you watch "Sixty Minutes" on television?
The article "Narcissism" was in *Psychology Today*.

Quotation marks are used for direct speech, as explained in Lesson 20. Do not use quotation marks to emphasize words (but underlining a word is all right to emphasize it). Quotation marks are used around words or expressions such as slang terms, special terms coined by another writer, and other special senses. Here are some examples:

Abraham Maslow calls a healthy personality a "self-actualizing" person, and
   Carl Rogers uses the term "fully functioning."
Rainy days make most people feel "blue."
Accidents are more likely to occur on these "critical days."
The boy was shot with an "unloaded" gun.

Either quotation marks or underlining may be used for words or expressions
used as their own names. Examples:

The word "smog" was created by combining "smoke" and "fog."
The words *am* and *is* are forms of the verb *be.* (Words underlined by hand
   or on a typewriter are italicized in print.)
Many teenagers sprinkle their sentences with "you know."

Underlining (italics) may also be used for emphasizing words, but do not overdo
this kind of emphasis (or any other kind).

We heard what he *said,* but what did he *mean?* (Good use of emphasis for
   contrast.)

I *really* liked your singing, Nancy; it's the *best* I've *ever* heard. (Overdone
   and unnecessary emphasis.)

Exercise V. Use underlining or quotation marks as needed in the following
sentences:

1 A review of the book The Andromeda Strain appeared in Newsweek Magazine.

2 The TV comedy Mork and Mindy made fun of expressions like tease my hair.

3 If he's so honest, why did Honest John cheat on his income tax?

4 Frost's poem The Road Not Taken is about choices.

5 The song Old Man River came from the musical play Showboat.

6 Never use quotation marks for emphasis, and I mean never.

7 Larry thinks The Los Angeles Times is as good as The New York Times.

8 One student misread John Donne's line Death be not proud as saying Death is not proud, completely changing the meaning.

9 Like snow and Santa Claus, the song White Christmas comes back every year.

10 George Eliot's novel Silas Marner and her poem The Choir Invisible are still being read today.

22

Hyphens to Join and Separate Words

Rule 1 Use hyphens (-) to make compound words.

Rule 2 Use hyphens to divide words between syllables at the end of a line.

Compound words are two or more words put together to make one, like these:

twenty-one	all-purpose	filter-tip
sit-in	self-made	ex-wife
put-down	motor-driven	Afro-American
two-year-old	world-shaking	part-time
mother-in-law	next-to-last	left-handed
sisters-in-law	down-to-earth	nine-tenths

Words like *postman* and *basketball* started out as *post-man* and *basket-ball* but now are written without the hyphen. Because words change over time, some compound words may be written two ways for a while (like *co-operate* or *cooperate*), and you may need to check a dictionary for the acceptable spelling.

Whenever you want two words to be a unit, join them with a hyphen. This is important for adjectives when the two words would not modify the noun separately:

an *air-conditioned* building (not an *air* building or a *conditioned* building)
a *million-dollar* man (not a *million* man or a *dollar* man)

But you do not need hyphens when the adjectives could modify the noun separately:

a pretty new dress (both a *pretty* dress and a *new* dress)

Ordinarily, we do not join adverbs to adjectives with hyphens. We say "a partly finished paper," not "a partly-finished paper." But sometimes the adverb *well* is used in compound words, as in "well-written play," "well-marked book," or a "sense of well-being."

Hyphens to Divide

Hyphens are also used to divide a word at the end of a line when the whole word won't fit. Divide only between syllables; never divide words of one syllable like *thought, reached, stretched,* and so on. (Basically, a syllable is a vowel sound and the consonant sounds that go with it—the unit of rhythm or number of "beats" in a word.) A dictionary always shows the places where words can be divided, like these:

pho-to-graph   pho-tog-ra-pher   mis-lead-ing   health-y

There are many rules for dividing at certain points in a word, but generally you will be safe if you follow these guidelines:

1. Keep letter combinations like *th* and *ph* in the same syllables; otherwise, you can usually divide between two consonants like this:

    aw-ful   en-ter-tain   dir-ty   in-form

2. Keep suffixes like *-ing* and *-er* together; otherwise, you can usually divide after a vowel when you don't have two consonants together.

    lo-cal   pro-tect   bit-ing
    fi-nal   pa-per   writ-er

Pronunciation does make a difference, as in pho-TOG-ra-phy and PHO-to-graph. So check your dictionary when you aren't sure where to divide.

Exercise W. Make compound adjectives out of the following phrases, as in the example.

Example: a person of middle age = a middle-aged person

1 A college that takes two years

2 A budget of a billion dollars

3 A salesman of cars that are used

4 A citizen born as a native

5 A suit that looks good

6 An apartment with two bedrooms

7 A program that trains tutors

8 A politician who waves the flag

9 Walls covered with ivy

10 A celebration that lasts all day

Divide the following words, showing all places where hyphens could go to divide each of them at the end of a line. If you can't divide, write the unbroken one-syllable word.

Example: information = in-for-ma-tion

11	nation	16	healthiest
12	excitement	17	preacher
13	contest	18	liked
14	following	19	tomorrow
15	taught	20	homelike

Appendix

DO NOT WRITE IN THIS BOOK

STUDENT RECORD FORM

Name (Last) _____ (First) _____

Phone _____ Class Days and Time _____ Instructor _____

Counselor _____ How Many Units Are You Carrying? _____

Put initials in the blanks under "done" when the work is completed.

CONTROLLED COMPOSITIONS

Date	Number	Done	Redone	Date	Number	Done	Redone

CREATING ASSIGNMENTS AND/OR FREE WRITING

Date	Number	Done	Date	Number	Done	Date	Number	Done

INDEX